MOVING?

HOW TO HIRE A MOVING COMPANY AND/OR MOVE YOURSELF

MOVING?

HOW TO HIRE A MOVING COMPANY AND/OR MOVE YOURSELF

By
D.L. Watrous

Books may be purchased in quantity and/or special sales by contacting the publisher by email/phone at
customerservice@moveco.net (800) 590-0928
Published by: Create Space
Photos by: Deposit photos Inc, Moveco.net, Wikipedia and D.L Watrous
Cover Design by: Create Space
Copy Editing by: Kasidee Rumsey

Moving? How to Hire a Moving Company and/or Move Yourself

Library of Congress

ISBN-13:
978-1979582193

ISBN-10:
197958219X

1. moving company 2. movers 3. moving 4. house relocation 5. how to move yourself 6. home relocation 7.diy movers 8. Dallas movers 9. Texas movers 10. moveco.net

Second Edition

TABLE OF CONTENTS

Chapter One
The Ease of a Professional Move

Chapter Two
The Do It Your Self Mover

Chapter Three
Moving Quotes

Chapter Four
Moving Companies

Chapter Five
The Art of Packing

Chapter Six
Before Move Day

Chapter Seven
Move Day

Chapter Eight
After Your Move

Chapter Nine
Don't Be a Horror Story

Chapter Ten
The Rich History of The Moving Industry

About Us

APPENDICES

1. Your Rights and Responsibilities

2. Government and Over Sight Organization Contact Information

3. Rental Truck and Moving Supply Contact Information

4. Helpful Numbers

5. Change Your Address Information

6. Household Goods Inventory Sheet

7. Tips and Tricks Before Move Day

8. Contact Information

9. Our Standards

INTRODUCTION

This little book is about knowing the right questions to ask when hiring a professional moving company and/or moving yourself. If you do not know how the moving industry operates, it is easy to make assumptions and have misunderstandings with the rental truck company or your moving company.

Like with most things, knowledge is power. We will cover common pitfalls and mistakes people sometimes make and how to avoid them. We will talk about the different kinds of moving quotes and the different classes of moving companies.

We will cover the complex and sometimes confusing subject of moving insurance.

We will cover how to properly pack a moving truck and what moving supplies are generally needed.

We will cover packing boxes, everything from crystal and china to clothes and pictures.

We will cover the moving experience. How it should be, as well as the horror stories, and how to avoid them.

We will finish with a brief history of the moving industry and its unique place in our society.

There is useful information in the appendix on a variety of topics from an inventory sheet to change of address information.

More and more DIYers are hiring a professional moving company to move the "big stuff". DIYers often will move all the small items and call the pros for the items that need more care, furniture dollies, and strong men. The point being you do not have to do everything yourself or hire a full-service mover to do everything. There is a lot of middle ground. Moving the small items yourself and hiring the pros for the big stuff is becoming a more common solution to fit your budget and save your back.

Of course, you can hire a full service moving company to do everything, so you do not have to lift a finger. Just make sure you pick the right moving company. This book will help you know how to do the right research and pick the best moving company for your needs.

People have many questions and concerns when it comes to relocating everything under their roof. The top five questions and concerns are, in order of importance:

1. Is the price competitive?
2. Will the movers show up on time?
3. Will my move price change once all my belongings are in the truck?
4. What if something gets damaged?
5. What about the quality of the moving crew that is working in my home, around my personal possessions, and precious family?

The information in this book can save you time, money, and heart ache.

MOVING?

HOW TO HIRE A MOVING COMPANY AND/OR MOVE YOURSELF

CHAPTER ONE
THE EASE OF A PROFESSIONAL MOVE

Moving is one of the most stressful of life events. Just below death, divorce, bankruptcy, and illness, but it doesn't have to be. A professional move performed by a quality crew will make all the difference.

Just like most decisions in life, information and knowledge will make all the difference in making the right decision in whether or not to hire a moving company. As well as, what moving company out of the thousands that are out there to choose from. Moving furniture is hard manual labor which requires a unique skill set.

There are enough questions about the moving process to fill a much larger book than the small book you hold in your hands. Here are just a few questions that you should be considering when making your decision on which moving company to hire.

"What classes of moving companies are there? Why is there such a dramatic range in quote prices for the exact same move? What is included in a moving quote? What are the pros and cons of hourly vs. itemized moving quotes? What is an "estimate" vs. a "not to exceed" moving quote? How much money do I really save if I pack myself?

"What about insurance? What is the difference between insurance and a guarantee? What does GL and cargo insurance cover? What is with this "supplemental insurance" I keep hearing about? Who pays the deductible if there is a claim? What kind of coverage do I really need?
How are the movers screened?

"What kind of men am I letting into my home and around my family? How long will my move take? I want my movers to be fast but not at the expense of being careful. My friend moved twice in the last two years. One move took three days, the other eight hours, what gives?"

When you do not have all the answers, anxiety and stress is a normal emotional response.

Research shows when most folks are asked to recommend a moving company, they start by saying who not to use. Reliving a bad moving experience in the process. People tend to be loyal to the companies they trust; the companies that treated them fairly in the past. A reputable mover will get most of their business from repeat customers and referrals.

LIFE IS UNPREDICTABLE, MAKE SURE YOUR MOVE ISN'T

What is the foundation of a professional stress-free move? Good communication and delivering on those expectations. Every move is unique with its own set of challenges. Moving your precious household goods is not like moving freight where everything is standard, sized, and sitting on a pallet.

A highly skilled crew is a must for a damage free move. Loading a moving truck is a lot like playing Tetris, with every piece of furniture being wrapped and padded first. Like most skilled trades, experience makes all the difference. It will not matter how good the moving company is if you get a bad crew. The three main factors that will affect the happiness of your moving experience are: a good company, a fair moving quote, and a competent crew. Please note it's best to reserve your move date two weeks in advance, if not sooner.

Reputable moving companies do not over book and their calendars fill up quickly, especially at the end of the month.

Make sure you know what your moving quote includes and that you have reviewed the written proposal/contract. Be sure the moving company you've selected is flexible with inventory adjustments and/or move conditions. Make sure last-minute services have upfront pricing without penalties or surcharges. Sometimes your friend that was so happy you gave them your old sofa set just doesn't understand the importance of deadlines or move dates or answering their phone. Maybe at the last minute your husband decides to swing by the old storage unit to make use of this extra manpower and large moving truck. Sometimes you may need additional services.

Life can be unpredictable, make sure your moving company isn't.

PROFESSIONAL PACKING SERVICES

It is 8 AM the day before your move. There is a knock at your door. The clean-cut packing crew is wearing matching uniforms. You know based on your prior research that this company does background checks, drug tests, and has vetted the references of each packing/moving crew member. It does not matter how skilled your mover is, if you would not trust him in your house. After introductory courtesies, you invite them into your house and do a quick walk through with the crew leader, identifying concerns and answering questions. All boxes will be labeled based on where you will want the items at your new address. As you have pointed out individual rooms, the crew leader has taken note: master bedroom, Emilie's bedroom, Wesley's bedroom, laundry, kitchenette, et cetera. Meanwhile, the other members of the crew have brought in piles of new crisp boxes and packing supplies.

There is packing tape, shrink wrap, bubble wrap, wardrobe boxes, 1.5 cubic ft. book boxes, 3.1 cubic ft. median boxes, and 4.5 cubic ft. large boxes, 4.5 cubic ft. dish packs and picture/mirror boxes. You're asked to sign the contract before they start. The contract is familiar, it is the same proposal you reviewed when you reserved your move date.

The crew gets to work. Carefully wrapping all breakable items, and labeling the boxes, "fragile" or "glass". Books and heavier items are packed in 1.5 cubic ft. book boxes. Lighter items are packed in larger boxes. Hanging clothes are packed in wardrobe boxes which are like mini closets with a metal bar to hang the clothes.

You are on hand to answer any questions the crew may have, one of which is, "What should be packed in your priority boxes?" The stuff you will need immediately after the move. Things like coffee, cups, coffee pot for you, tooth brushes, and pajamas for the kids. If what you need most is identified now, packed, and labeled, you will not be searching every box on the move night just to put the kids to bed. The first day in your new home can be kind of chaotic. A few well packed "priority boxes" can make all the difference.

The phone rings a few hours later, it is the moving company's office. The lady on the phone just wants to know if everything is all right and going smoothly. She asks if you have any questions. She then confirms the time the move crew will be there in the morning. It was just a courtesy call.

As the day progresses, neat stacks of boxes about four to five feet tall fill the house. Each box is labeled with its contents and what room it is destined for at the new house. Boxes that are sealed with tape are about forty percent stronger than boxes that are just folded. Every box is sealed with tape.

As the day comes to a close, your entire home is packed by professionals. The crew leader does a walk through with you to double check that everything that needed to be packed, was indeed packed. Meanwhile, the crew picks up any trash, empty tape rolls, box bundle binders, et cetera.

The crew leader asks you to sign the move contract acknowledging the packing services performed. He leaves you with a copy of the updated move contract with actual box numbers, as well as his business card. Goodbyes are said, and the crew departs.

You look around with great relief. What would have taken an average family (with friends helping) over a week of exhausting work and multiple trips to the box store, has been completed in just one day. You think to yourself this is the way to prep for a move. You are ready for the movers tomorrow!

MOVE DAY

The phone rings, it's the movers. They tell you they are about 15 minutes away, and will arrive on time. You think it is thoughtful of the driver to give you a courtesy call. You are ready. Everything is in sealed boxes with labeled contents and where the box will go at the new house. The desk drawers and armoires are empty, but you left your clothes in the dressers and chest of drawers. They said clothes were ok to leave in the drawers, but any big furniture had to be emptied like the armoire and high boy.

The company name and logo are clearly visible on the side of the moving truck. The driver introduces himself and the moving crew. You recognize the driver from the email you received yesterday from the moving company, confirming the date and time, as well as, which driver has been assigned to your moving crew.

The driver has the exact same inventory list that you were given when you received your moving quote a month ago. After a walk through where you answer any questions the driver may have about the particulars of this move, you sign the moving contract. You feel you are on the same page as your moving crew. The best way to achieve great customer service is to avoid any miscommunication.

The truck is stocked with professional moving equipment and stacks of moving quilts. Rubberized non-marking dollies are brought in, as well as moving straps and shrink wrap. Floor protection is laid down and the door jam protectors are installed.

It does not take long for the crew to clear out the living room and entryway. Stacks of boxes roll out to the truck effortlessly. The clutter of a packed house is quickly disappearing. The movers disassemble the headboards and footboards of the beds. The mirrors are unscrewed off the dressers. After the washer and dryer are disconnected, you are asked to view the washer outlet to confirm for yourself that there are no leaks. After all, you are responsible for the house's plumbing, not the moving company. You go out to the moving truck to see how much space is still left. You are surprised how much they are able to fit into the moving truck.   Every piece of furniture is wrapped in a moving pad. All the different shapes and sizes fitting together like a puzzle. Boxes are filling all the places on top of and in-between the furniture. This is quite an impressive pack job.

Once the truck is loaded, the driver does a walk through with you. A final check to make sure nothing is missed. A padlock is installed on the back door of the moving truck. The driver confirms your new address. The driver asks if you would prefer meeting at your new address or just have them follow you. You choose to have them follow you. You drive extra slow on the starts and stops. Moving trucks take it slow and easy on the road to minimize the bumps and road vibrations.

At your new home, a walk through is conducted so the crew will know the "names" of the various rooms. This way the boxes will be placed in the correct room. Floor protection and door guards are then installed. You are asked to "direct traffic" and make sure each piece of furniture is exactly where you want it in the first place. No reason to have to move things around again when you have all this manpower now. It is such a hassle to have to move things around later.

After the truck is unloaded, you are asked to inspect the moving truck. All the moving pads are in two neat stacks with the dollies strapped to the wall. You know for sure that no items were accidently left in the truck. You also know only your belongings were in this moving truck during this move.

You're asked to write down on the contract any damages you have noticed. There was none. You sign the contract completing your move and tip the crew.

You are happy with your moving experience. You post a comment on the company website as well as your favorite review board; Yelp, Yahoo, Google, or Angie's List for example. You also plan to refer this company to your friends, family, and coworkers.

The next day you receive a survey in your email inbox asking, "How was your moving experience?" You are pleased to leave positive comments.

A move done right makes life that much easier.

CHAPTER TWO
THE "DO IT YOURSELF" MOVER

There is a lot to consider when moving yourself. You need to rent a truck, rent moving pads, buy rope/straps, and rent or buy moving dollies. Everything you need to move yourself safely needs to be in place well before move day. The actual move is just one piece of the puzzle. There are a ton of move related issues that will require your attention.

The days leading up to your move can make you feel like a juggler in a circus. There are utilities that need to be changed, house closings to attend, documents that need to be signed, and kids to enroll in school. Moving is a full-time job before you even pack your first box. You will save money by moving yourself, but a professional moving crew sure can make life easier.

When you're planning on moving yourself, organization is the key. You will need a written schedule and a checklist to make sure everything that needs to be done gets done on time. Friends need to be drafted, both for move day and to help with the packing. Packing is something that, for the most part, can be done at your convenience but must be completed before move day. It is recommended to start packing two weeks before move day. Everyone takes longer packing their own items. It is a curious fact that professional movers will pack a stranger's household goods faster than they would their own. The reason being, each item is tied to a memory, so it is more than just wrapping and boxing. It's remembering your past one item at a time.

The main objective when moving yourself should be, not to get hurt. It is far easier to replace a piece of furniture than to replace your back. A potential back injury is the number one reason to hire a moving company. If you are moving yourself, invest in a back brace and lift with your legs. Give yourself more time than you think you'll need. Moving yourself has a way of dragging on and on.

One of the main problems folks have when moving themselves, is the "lowered standard" and the "cutting corners" that lead to accidents and damages. For example, professional movers will not move boxes that are open or folded. Boxes must be sealed with tape. People that move themselves don't seem to think twice about carrying out open boxes to the moving truck that are overflowing. DIY movers also do not seem to use enough moving pads on their furniture, resulting in damage. If you're planning on moving yourself, don't let this happen to you. Use plenty of moving blankets.

You can be successful with the right preparation and the right knowledge. It only takes moving yourself once to appreciate the effort that a professional mover puts forth. If you hire a professional moving company, do your research, know what standard to demand.

RENTING THE MOVING TRUCK

As soon as you know your actual move date, the first thing to do is reserve your rental truck. U-Haul, Penske, and Budget are all good companies to use when moving, but they do run short of trucks at the end of the month. That is especially true of the 24 ft.-26 ft. moving trucks, which is the truck you will need if you are moving a household. The truck can be reserved online with a credit card. Call the rental truck company a few days before the move just to make sure they actually have the physical truck on hand.

A 24-ft. rental truck is 1,536 cubic feet, while a typical professional moving truck is 2,160 cubic feet, but the real difference is the skill to pack a truck that comes from years of experience. It is not uncommon for the professional mover to fit twice the amount of furniture and boxes in this truck than the average DIY mover. This is not a big deal though, if you have chosen to move yourself. It is far better to make more trips than to spend an exorbitant amount of time trying to maximize your 1,536 cubic ft. worth of space. The important thing to remember is that the truck must be packed in a way so the furniture cannot slide around and shift. Every piece of furniture must be wrapped with a moving blanket. Use boxes as space fillers. Make use of ropes and straps to attach items to the walls of the truck. Keep heavy items at the bottom of the load, and stack light items on the top.

It is a good idea to know the additional cost if you need to keep the truck for a couple extra days. Just like Blockbuster's notorious late fees (pre-Netflix), the truck rental fees can sometimes exceed the original cost of the rental. Some savvy DIYers will add a few extra days to the rental agreement when first reserving their truck. Adding days to the truck rental is much cheaper when they are added three weeks before the move, than the day of the move.

When you return the rental truck, make sure to fill the fuel tank and to sweep it out to avoid any extra fees. It is also a good idea to take a photograph of the rental truck before starting your move, as well as, after you have unloaded and cleaned out the truck. This will give you proof of any damages that occurred before you rented the truck or any damages that occurred during your move. Sometimes folks get their credit card charged for truck damages without notice. An email with before and after pictures will get any bogus charges refunded.

MOVING EQUIPMENT AND SUPPLIES

You don't need everything in the professional movers' tool kit, but you do need some essentials. Where you rented your moving truck is a good place to look for rental dollies, as well as, other moving supplies. There are also moving supply stores available where all the pros shop.

The first thing you will need is a box dolly or hand

truck to move boxes. This type of dolly is also convenient to move furniture, just make sure it is padded. Almost all rental hand trucks are NOT padded. Almost all professional hand trucks ARE padded.

The second kind of dolly that you will need is a four-wheel dolly. Again, you can rent one, but in my opinion it is well worth the sixty dollars to buy a professional one. A good four-wheel dolly is indispensable to a smooth move. Furniture can be tipped on its rubberized pads and rolled around tight corners. Heavy items can be maneuvered with ease using this type of dolly.

The third kind of dolly you will need is an appliance dolly to move the fridge, freezer, washer, and dryer. This is a heavy-duty dolly that has a ratchet strap attached, to make sure the appliance is secure. This dolly is expensive, but can easily be rented.

Next you need rope, straps, and shrink wrap. Not only do you need to tie items to the wall of the truck, but you also need to wrap and tie the drawers and doors of your furniture. Dressers, chests, china cabinets, buffets, nightstands, and desks all need to be tied to prevent accidental opening. Many damages have occurred when a dolly operator rolls out a piece of furniture only to have the door swing open and crash into the concrete driveway.

All packing needs to be done before move day. Let me say that again, all the boxes need to be packed and sealed before move day. There are a lot of supply stores that sell boxes at a discount. All reputable moving companies sell boxes and will deliver them to you at little or no cost. The truck rental companies sell boxes as well. Check the return policy before you buy moving supplies, just in case you need to make a return or exchange. The right moving equipment and moving supplies is a must to make your move go smoothly.

PIZZA AND BEER

There is a lot to take into consideration when you are asking your friends to help you move. The more stuff you have, the harder it is to get your friends to commit. Gone are the days when all your stuff would fit in the back of your friends' pick up, an SUV, two jeeps and a Honda Civic. Now you have to rent a moving truck. Not just any truck, but the biggest truck that can legally be rented with a class C driver's license. Note: If any of

your friends plan to drive the moving truck they will need to be on the insurance and rental agreement.

The protocol is pizza and beer on move day, and the obligation to reciprocate when said friend moves in the future. Kind of a "one day I will ask of you a favor."

Over the years I have heard thousands of stories of friends bailing out at the last minute, "I was on my way, but my car broke down!" "I have the flu." "My grandmother is ill." "My boss called me in to work, sorry buddy." It's even got as bad as friends not answering their phone on move day and using the excuse the next time they see you, "Sorry, I flaked." like it's no big deal. Your polite friends will at least have a preexisting, "I can't get out of a previous engagement," that's conveniently scheduled on your move day.

If you are using a moving company just to move all the big items and using your friends to move all the small stuff and boxes, here is a suggestion: make sure the moving company that you hired will add items at the last minute just in case your friends flake. It is always a good idea to have a backup plan.

Some friends are better at packing boxes then actual moving that requires the heavy lifting, delegate accordingly. Make sure that all the packing is done before move day. It is way too stressful to still be packing boxes while you are trying to load the truck.

What about the scuffs and scrapes? Accidents tend to happen when working with nonprofessionals, especially when your friend just chugged a beer to wash down his pizza. You can't expect your friend to pay for your TV if he accidently drops it. Same goes for the walls. If a table corner bumps the wall and knocks out a small, or not so small, chunk of sheetrock, you most likely will just have to smile and fix it yourself. He is here to help his friend, so you can't necessarily get upset. He doesn't have the experience of moving furniture eight hours a day for the last two years. (The time it takes to become a truly proficient furniture mover.)

The main issue to consider is what if somebody gets hurt? Does your friend have health insurance? Will it cover them not being able to return to work? Will they expect you to pay the doctor bills or lost wages? Friends don't sue friends for personal injury, do they? It's happened before in the past. A friendship can easily be ruined over a move gone bad. You have to ask yourself, what are the costs and risks of free labor?

DAY LABORERS AND CRAIG'S LIST

There are other ways to get the manpower you need without relying on your friends. You can post an ad for day laborers or find your local day labor pool. In fact, some "low cost" moving companies hire additional staff by using day labor. There are questions you need to ask yourself before you proceed with this low-cost labor source. Any reputable moving company conducts a background check and drug test when hiring movers. Will you research the laborers you hire?

Men with addictions or a questionable past have a

 tendency to work for cash on a daily basis vs. holding down a full-time job. If you are concerned about the type of people you are bringing into your home and around

your family, this might be an issue. Strangers for cash labor may have untold costs.

Experience also must be considered. Moving is a trade that requires a unique set of skills. When someone hauls trash one day and roofing shingles the next day, why would they have the skill to move your cherry wood dresser and stainless-steel fridge today? Moving is not just grunt work; moving furniture is highly skilled, hard manual labor. You can't train someone in one day. Why would you want to train someone on your dime with your stuff? It is possible to hire skilled labor on a daily basis. Hire a professional moving company. If you are not using a respectable moving company, you will need to vet the men yourself.

Insurance is a big deal when you are moving. If one of your day laborers gets injured, who is responsible? If you don't have an independent contractor's agreement, then you are the one held responsible. Will your homeowner's insurance defend you in court against a personal injury lawsuit? There is a lot to consider when you hire strangers to come and work in your home. Make sure you are asking these questions before your move day.

Furniture getting damaged is normally the main concern when hiring day laborers, but you can see it is not nearly as vital as some of the points we just covered. To be clear, you are responsible for any damages your day laborers cause. If they drop your TV or scratch your dining room table, are you going to ask them to pay for it? Will you take it out of their wages? What good is $100 wages on a $1200 TV? It is doubtful you would want to stiff a day laborer anyway. They know where you live, they've been in your home, and they have a good idea of where all your items are located. Just pay the day laborer for their services, and think of it as a learning experience.

How much do you really save with day labor vs. getting the job done right with a professional moving company? Only you can answer that question.

THREE LEVELS OF SERVICE

Hiring a professional moving company to pack your entire home, move your belongings to your new residence, and then unpack every box for you is the extreme package. That's what we call "living the good life," when it comes to household relocation.

The other extreme is doing everything yourself. You can find some middle ground where how much you spend and how much you save make the most sense to you. Value is where quality meets the lowest price and you can get the level of service that you want and need.

Moving your home can be broken down into three levels of service. The first level is the full-service move. This includes having the moving company of your choice pack all of your belongings, then unpack for you at your new home. The first step in saving money is unpacking yourself. You can save even more money by packing some of your items yourself, leaving breakable and hard items to the professionals.

The second level of service is packing all the boxes yourself, but leaving the moving to the professionals. The cost of a move can often be cut in half if you pack all of your boxes yourself. Packing requires no heavy lifting or furniture dollies. In fact, most people pack themselves and hire the movers for the actual move. On move day, all boxes must be sealed with tape. All furniture must be emptied; although, some moving companies let you leave your clothes in the chest of drawers and dressers.

The third level of service is where the moving company is hired to move just the big items. The two-man items, the pieces of furniture you want insured, and the items you would just feel better if the pros moved them. You and your posse of friends move all the small stuff, the one-man items. When you get an itemized quote just to move the big stuff, the moving price really falls through the floor.

When deciding whether to move yourself or hire a professional mover (or somewhere in between), consider the comparative advantage. How much is your time worth to you? How much is the risk worth? How much is the peace of mind worth? How much hassle do you want to eliminate? Some folks don't value their free time like they should. Time is your most precious resource. Time is a scarce resource with alternative uses.

With a professional moving company, your move will be fast and efficient. If anything gets damaged, the company will have guarantees and insurance to take care of the problem. If anyone gets hurt, you are not held responsible. You will not have to rely on friends or owe them a favor. You have enough on your plate with all that goes into moving to your new home.

CHAPTER THREE
MOVING QUOTES

When you are moving your family, there is a lot to consider. Most folks that decide to hire a professional moving company will get three to five quotes. Most people will do a Google search or pick up a phone book and pick the companies "that look good". Some may even do their research on the BBB and check the online testimonials. Price is usually the deciding factor. Few consider what is really included in a moving quote or what types of moving quotes there may be to choose from.

There are local, statewide, and nationwide moving companies. There are itemized, hourly, by the pound, by the cubic foot, and flat rate moves. Some services may be included in one company's quote, while another company charges extra for those same services. It is very common for what one company considers standard, another moving company may consider optional. "Caveat Emptor", buyer beware.

Understanding your move quote is the first step in a successful move. Different moving companies do things differently. It is your responsibility, as a customer, to compare quotes to see what may be the best choice for you and for your budget.

Moving everything in your home from point A to B is not the same as buying a TV or a toaster oven where you can buy the exact same item at multiple stores. Moving is a service industry that is tailor made to each customer, one move at a time. Each move is unique. Just like fingerprints, each person's belongings are unique to them.

Some moving quotes are easier to compare than others. Itemized quotes can be compared line by line. Hourly quotes, on the other hand, are harder to compare because the length of time the move takes will depend on the speed and skill of the crew.

The best way to compare moving quotes is to first sort them by type. Compare itemized to itemized and hourly to hourly. It is not uncommon to receive both itemized and hourly quotes by the same company. You also need to research the quality of the companies. Check the BBB, and make sure they are licensed with the state (Department of Transportation of the state you are currently living in.)

Review their insurance policy. Testimonials are also a great resource. Seeing what people have said about the moving companies that have actually moved with them can give you an idea of what to expect. A referral from a trusted friend or family member is by far the most powerful. Most folks will only get one quote from a company they were referred to, that's how much trust a referral can bring (vs. the three to five moving quotes).

On the other hand, some people can only recommend what moving companies not to use. Bad moving experiences can often scar a customer.

Insurance and guarantees are also important to review and can affect your move price, as well as, what recourse you have if something gets damaged.

Beware of third party moving quotes. I recommend only getting quotes from actual moving companies that will be conducting your move. There are brokers with awesome websites and aggressive salesmen. Internet brokers will book your move and then outsource the actual move to a moving company you may know nothing about. This happened to a friend of my wife. She had gotten a quote of $1500.00 to move from Dallas to Los Angeles. On her move day, the crew did not show up. She found out that the truck was two days behind schedule because they were "piggy backing" her load on a cross country run. Worse yet she found out the $1500.00 was just a deposit, a nonrefundable deposit. The crew wanted $4500.00 more in money orders or a cashier's check. She could have saved herself the trouble if she had carefully reviewed the quote. She ended up renting a U-Haul.

Understanding your move quote is a big part of making your move stress free. After you have selected a moving company and have your quote in hand, it is a good idea to reserve your move date at least two weeks ahead of time.

QUOTE TYPES

The itemized moving quote is the gold standard in moving quotes. You get a printed inventory list with all of your furniture, boxes, and miscellaneous items. The miles from your pickup address to your drop off address, as well as any extra stops are noted. Other conditions, such as long walks and stairs, are on the contract as well. You receive an exact price in writing based on your conditions and exact inventory. If you only wanted help with the big items, your inventory will reflect only the large items. You are in control with an itemized moving quote.

The best way to get an itemized quote is with an in-home estimate. Most reputable companies will provide this service at no charge. An in-home estimate takes about twenty minutes for a walk through of most homes. All of your furniture and conditions will be noted on a laptop or clipboard, and you will be given a written itemized furniture list with your move quote. If you would prefer the convenience of getting your quote online or by phone, you can list your own furniture and conditions; your itemized quote will be as accurate as your list.

The hourly move quote is not a binding exact price because by its very nature, it is a quote based on time not items. With an hourly moving quote, you pay for how long the movers are there, not by the items being moved. This creates a conflict of interest with dispatch. Good crews want to be on itemized moves and be paid for the work they actually do, not how much time they spend at your house. The skill that is gained with time and experience makes good crews much more efficient. Inexperienced and "slow" crews want to be on hourly moves because they get paid for how long they are "working," not the work that is actually being done. The dispatch office will put the "slow" crews on the hourly moves and the "fast" crews on the itemized moves; it just makes sense to do so. I don't care what a salesman will tell you when trying to "close" on an hourly move. Slow movers make more money by being slow on hourly moves and milking the clock.

I have been on many moves where the customer was amazed at how fast their move had been completed. I would always ask, "Was your last move hourly?" The answer was always, "yes." Don't be fooled by a low hourly quote, know what you are paying for upfront.

Other questions to ask when getting an hourly moving quote: "are there any hidden fees. Such as, a truck fee, fuel surcharge, travel time, and arrival fees." Some companies will start the clock the moment they leave their truck yard; therefore, charging you for the drive to your residence.

There are also quotes by the pound or by cubic feet. These quotes are usually for interstate moves, where the semi has multiple loads and will be weighed at the weigh stations. Van lines often use the per pound quote. Quotes by the pound or by cubic feet are based on an estimate. The true pounds/cubic foot is only known once the truck is loaded and/or weighed. Often folks are unaware they will have to pay for the additional tonnage.

"By the job quotes" are flat rates given by an in-home estimate only. The main advantage over the itemized quote is convenience. Normally the driver that did the flat rate quote will be conducting the actual move. You can also get a flat rate by the truck. This kind of quote can save you money on a long-distance move, but make sure you have an expert packing the truck. A professional can fit up to forty percent more furniture in the same size truck than a novice.

REQUESTING A MOVE QUOTE

There are several ways to get a moving quote. You can send an email 24/7 and wait for a response, or you can call and get your quote over the phone. Moving quotes given over the phone are okay for hourly moves or if you have a detailed inventory list to go over with the moving specialist. Most quality moving companies offer free in-home estimates. An in-home estimate is the best way to get an accurate moving quote.

A few moving companies have instant online quoting systems on their websites where you can get a guaranteed move price based on your inventory list and move conditions. Do not mistake "instant online quote" with an "online form" that is just emailed to the company. With the instant online quote, you get upfront pricing, and the quote price is displayed immediately. With the emailed form, you have to wait for a salesman to contact you.

You will find that there is a wide range of quote prices for seemingly the same move. In addition to how far you are moving and how much stuff you have, the quality and reputation of the moving company play a factor, as well as the skill and experience of the moving crew. A "low ball" move quote that changes on the day of the move is not really a low price.

When you receive your move quote, the company should provide you with a "written proposal" with a "binding" or a "not to exceed" price. What your quote is based on should be in print, whether it is a detailed inventory list or an estimated number of hours. The moving company should also provide you with TXDOT's "Rights and Responsibilities," as well as, their insurance and written guarantee. Ask what the cancelation and rescheduling fees are, if any. Ask if a deposit is required and if it is refundable. Ask if there are any overtime charges if the crew works past a certain time.

It is always a good idea to request a list of additional services and fees. It is always a good idea to be prepared for unforeseen events. For example: what if the closing on your house is delayed? What is the wait charge if the moving crew has to sit around while you get your new keys? What if you need overnight storage on the truck? What if a traffic detour adds extra mileage? Being prepared is the best way to eliminate stress on move day.

Be careful of hidden charges. The better the moving company, the less hidden fees there are, and the more transparent the pricing. If a moving quote seems too good to be true, it probably is. Fair pricing is like buying oats. If you want nice clean oats, you will have to pay a fair price. If, however, you will be satisfied with oats that have already been through the horse, well that comes a little cheaper.

ADDITIONAL SERVICES

There are many additional services that can be requested that are not part of a standard move. There are also services that are standard with some companies but an extra charge for other moving companies. Additional services

needed at the drop off that were not were not listed on your original quote, will always add to your bill. For example: your move was based on moving to a ground level, but your new apartment is on the third floor. Reputable moving companies will make your quote as accurate as possible, but if you change your conditions, you have changed your own quote price.

Most reputable moving companies will have included in your quote price, the moving truck, arrival fee, and standard disassembly and reassembly. For example: taking mirrors off dressers, disassemble/reassemble of headboards and footboards, disassemble/reassemble of washer/dryers, and hutches off china cabinets, et cetera.

Complex disassembly of unique items and specialty items normally will cost more, but this, too, will be in your quote if you have had an in-home estimate or have reviewed the unique services that you required with the company. Any unique services should be detailed on your written quote. Some examples include, grand pianos, oversized glass tops, custom built entertainment centers, crating a nine-foot sailfish, crating a chandelier, et cetera. If you think you may own an item that is beyond standard, ask. Avoid any surprises on move day, both for you and the movers.

Auto and boat transport is also available with most moving companies with advanced notice.

All moving trucks should be equipped with basic tools, ample moving blankets, four-wheel dolly, appliance dolly, box dolly, rubber furniture bands, straps, and shrink wrap.

Floor plastic and door covers are standard with some moving companies. They are not available or an extra charge with other moving companies. You need to ask what is included in your moving quote.

A word of caution about hourly quotes that advertise "no charge for stairs, long walks, and shrink wrap."
While no charge may be technically true, long walks and stairs dramatically add to the amount of time an hourly crew will take to complete your move, hence adding to the total cost. Hourly crews also run up the clock, shrink wrapping everything for "free."

An additional service that can be a lifesaver, is short notice storage. If the unexpected happens, your closing is delayed, or your house is not ready to move in, know what storage options your moving company may offer. A full service moving company can get you out of a jam with a last-minute storage solution.

The only way to accurately compare moving quotes is to know what is standard and what is extra. The better the moving company, the more that is considered standard.

UNDERSTANDING INSURANCE

Liability insurance, cargo insurance, valuation, bonded, in-house guarantee, and 60 cents per pound. Trying to understand moving insurance can drive you nearly crazy. It is complicated. People think that they are covered only to find out that the movers insurance does not cover this or that or worse yet, that they only have protection at 60 cents per pound. There is much to consider before the first box is loaded onto the moving truck.

60 cents per pound is the industry standard that is mandated by government. Every licensed moving company has this basic coverage.

Cargo insurance covers your household goods while in transit. Meaning, while your furniture is in the truck and on the road. Cargo insurance includes theft, accidents, fire, et cetera.

Liability insurance covers damage to your home and/or if someone gets hurt by the actions of one of the movers. Example: The moving truck backed into your house.

Liability insurance does not cover flooding caused by faulty plumbing in your kitchen/laundry room. That would be your home owners' insurance. The condition of a house's plumbing is always the responsibility of the home owner.

Bonded covers any property that was stolen by the moving crew. Most service companies are bonded. This is the same kind of bonded that cable guys, maids, and movers have. The bond will only pay if there is an actual conviction proving that something was stolen.

It is much better to use a moving company that has quality crews in the first place. Ask if the company does a thorough background check and drug screenings.

Valuation is like insurance but without the underwriter. You pay the mover a premium, and if there is a damaged item, you pay a deductible before the movers repair or replace the damaged item. This is a common additional service with the national van lines. Valuations can be a good deal under the right circumstance.

Actual furniture insurance is rare in the moving business, but it is available, normally through a third party. You buy a policy, pay a premium, and if something gets damaged, you make a claim and pay the deductible. The adjuster is sent to your house to handle the repairs or offer you a settlement.

If you own anything of extraordinary value, you should buy supplemental insurance on a per item basis. People with art or antiques valued over $10,000 normally buy or already have this type of per appraised item insurance.

The in-house policy or guarantee is a company policy not backed by an insurance company. Some reputable moving companies offer to repair or replace anything that their movers happen to damage. Moving companies with poor or inexperienced crews simply cannot offer this kind of guarantee and hide behind the 60 cents per pound industry standard. The movers that repair or replace anything that their movers damage typically does itemized moves. Crews with the skill that comes from experience and have a record of minimal or no damages, prefer to work for a moving company that charges for what is actually done, not how long the move takes. In the moving industry, hourly movers and 60 cents per pound insurance go hand-in-hand.

In review, make sure that the moving company that you hire is licensed, bonded, and has both cargo and liability insurance. For small damages that are typical of a household move, get a moving company that has an in-house guarantee to repair or replace anything that their crew happens to damage. Not only will it be easier to settle a claim, the crew will be of much better quality, so you probably won't have any damages to worry about in the first place.

PACKING QUOTES

Some moving companies make packing quotes more complex than they need to be. There are two sides of the same coin when it comes to packing quotes. Packing supplies and the labor used to actually pack the boxes. Almost all packing quotes are estimates. It is almost impossible to guess just how many boxes will be packed until all is said and done. Understanding the packing quote is essential.

Some companies charge hourly rates for the packing crew and itemize the boxes, tape, bubble wrap, and packing paper used. They then charge you full retail for all the packing supplies. You wind up paying about the same as if you bought your boxes at U-Haul or perhaps even more. It is easy to run up a $500 plus bill just for the packing supplies.

As with all hourly quotes, the quality and speed of the packing crew will affect how long it takes to pack your house, as well as, how much you pay.

Some companies charge a flat rate per box packed and still charge you retail for the boxes and packing paper. The better moving companies charge a flat rate per box, and include the box, packing paper, tape, and bubble wrap. Free packing supplies means you won't be nickeled and dimed over every roll of tape and sheet of packing paper. The movers buy the boxes wholesale anyway. Free boxes and packing supplies lets you know they are not profiting on the cardboard and the packers are earning their money by providing you with quality service.

An itemized packing quote is based on the estimated number of boxes that you will need packed. Ask how much any additional boxes would be to pack, and if less boxes are packed then quoted how that would that affect the price.

Ask about insurance and company guarantees on boxes packed by the movers. Boxes packed by the customer normally do not carry the same protection, "contents unknown".

It is common for people to request a partial pack job only using the professionals to pack up the kitchen and other breakable items. Some folks use the packers as a backup plan to pack whatever their friends and family were not able to finish. Make sure your packing quote is flexible and you only pay for the work that is actually performed.

A by the box flat rate is the best packing quote to get. A typical by the box flat rate includes all the supplies: packing paper, tape, bubble wrap, and the box. Typical pricing is:

- $8 for 1.5 cubic ft. box
- $9 for a 3.1 cubic ft. box
- $12 for a 4.2 cubic ft. box
- $15 for dish packs
- $15 for wardrobes
- $10 for picture/mirror boxes

Of course, each company sets their own pricing.

You can save a lot of money by packing yourself, but if you want to save yourself the stress and hire a professional packing crew, know what your quote includes. Never be afraid to ask questions. You are the customer, and the moving business is a service industry.

CHAPTER FOUR
MOVING COMPANIES

There are thousands of moving companies to choose from. Some advertise the lowest price, while others emphasize quality of service. Some moving companies have been around for over a hundred years, while others just bought their first truck yesterday.

You cannot compare moving quotes without comparing moving companies.

The reputation of the moving company is the first thing to consider when hiring a furniture mover. That is why referrals from friends and family members are so powerful. When someone you trust recommends a company, you generally know what to expect. Most folks are happy when their expectations are met.

People like to do business with people they like and feel they can trust. The nice sales woman on the phone that got you such a great "deal" is not going to be moving you.

Don't let the likeability of a professional salesperson that you will never meet again cloud your judgement. You are hiring movers to come into your house and move everything you own, move your family's worldly possessions. The man that did your in-home estimate is probably not going to be on the moving crew.

The quality of the moving company and the moving crews is what is important. Sales people do not stand behind service guarantees, companies do.

Many people have purchased a car because they liked the salesman. Many people have gotten stuck with a bad moving company because a charismatic sales associate made them feel at ease.

There are lots of questions to ask when considering potential moving companies. The top five concerns most families have are:

1. Is the price competitive?
2. Will the movers show up on time?
3. Will my price change once all my stuff is in the truck?
4. What if something gets damaged?
5. What is the quality of the moving crew that is working in my home, around my family?

Do your research, know what to expect. Even though business practices are as wide and varied as the company owners, most moving companies fall into seven categories.

CHUCK AND A TRUCK

Anyone can start a moving company. Put an ad on Craig's List, grab a buddy, and rent a truck.

The government requires moving companies to be licensed with the State's Department of Transportation (DOT). Without a valid DOT number, the moving company is breaking the law. It is easy to go online and check out a moving company's DOT number and make sure it is current. You can also view the insurance, view bond filings, and see if there are any complaints. (see appendix)

Do not do business with an illegal moving company. Illegal movers are where most of the horror stories come from. Criminals posing as movers, ready to steal your personal property, hold your belongings hostage, and extort you.

There are a multitude of advantages to dealing with a moving company that is licensed, bonded, and insured.

There is nothing wrong with a one truck startup, that runs their company on the road with a cell phone. Lots of one crew operations are run above board. Just make sure they have met state requirements and are legal.

When you select your mover, do your research. Reputations are gold in the moving industry. Reputations take time to earn. It takes time and experience to become a good furniture mover. Companies build their reputations on the crews one move at a time.

People are sometimes blinded by a low price. If the movers don't show up, show up late, items get damaged or they increase your move price, what are you going to tell your friends? "When I called the ad on Craig's List, Chuck said it was going to be $39 per hour." Your friends will ask how your move went. People are always on the lookout for good movers.

At the very least, hire a legal moving company. It is preferred to avoid the, "fly by nights" and hire a company with a reputation to protect.

The illegal small-time mover is rarely prosecuted with the laws already on the books. They come and go with each moving season. Being a mover one day, picking up side jobs the next. Often these companies have no history and are impossible to research. You may as well rent a truck, hire some day laborers and be your own "moving company for a day."

BUDGET/APT. MOVERS

The main selling point of this category of moving company is often the low price. Budget, Apts, Apartments, A1, A+, AAA and Best are often part of their name. Unlike some guy and a rental truck, these are real moving companies, so it's easy to research them with the BBB. They are normally licensed and meet the state requirements of 60 cents per pound insurance.

The trucks are often geared for smaller moves like apartments. Often, they use pickups to pull cargo trailers. This category of moving companies rarely performs interstate moves. They rarely do in-home estimates and most of their moves are booked over the telephone. Salesmen have flexibility and will often "cut deals." Make sure everything you want moved is listed. Same day add-ons are normally priced at a premium.

Budget movers do a lot of hourly moves, but the quality of the crew will determine how long the actual move will take.

People usually get what they pay for, but sometimes overpay for poor service. Do not let any work be performed without a written contract stating a maximum cost. Finding out the cost of your move after the truck is loaded, is finding out too late.

MOVE FOR FREE

Apartment locators and apartment complexes often run specials where they will move you for free. It is always nice to get something for free, but the old age saying is, "there is no such thing as a free lunch." This definitely rings true when talking about moving specials.

The money being paid to the mover on your behalf is generally for a set inventory list. If you have additional items you will have to pay extra if you want the add ons moved.

The mover will show up with a preprinted inventory list for your "free" move. You can then negotiate the cost to move everything else. Get the list before hand and know what is included.

As with any company, always go over the moving quote proposal before move day while you still have options. Sales gimmicks are just that, gimmicks. You could tell the apt. locator/apt. complex you would prefer to receive a check and you will hire your own moving company. Quality always suffers when you have no choice in who you hire. Most "move for free" deals are contracted with budget/apt. class moving companies.

People who think they are getting a "free" move often don't even know the name of the moving company until move day. How do you suppose to do your due diligence? "Free" often causes a cognitive shortcut. This makes you believe you have nothing to worry about, and you're given the idea that "it's taken care of" while in reality, we should be even more vigilant.

NATIONAL VAN LINES

National van lines move people across the country and across the world. They have contracts with the military, government (general services), as well as, large corporations. They are the 800-pound gorilla in the moving industry. The van lines are the polar opposite to "Chuck and a truck." There is no question, they have the legal authority to move furniture.

The national van lines set the industry standard. The van lines carry very high limits on their general liability, but their cargo insurance for regular damage is set at the industry standard, 60 cents per pound per item. Most van lines offer to sell additional insurance or valuation.

Some van lines are better than others, so do your research. The in-home estimate is the preferred method to receive a quote. Once the semi is loaded and the truck is weighed, you will know the actual weight and price of your move. Ask ahead of time what the additional cost per pound will be.

A large portion of corporate relocations are contracted with the national carriers. If your company is moving you, the cost of your move is between the van line and your company. I have met many people that had no idea what their move actually cost. "The company paid for it," they would say.

Most van lines are very professional, use large trucks, have experienced crews, but are kind of expensive if you're paying for the move out of your own pocket. On the other hand, they can be very competitive on long distance moves. If you can be flexible on your move date, then they can piggyback your load on a cross-country truck.

LOCAL INDEPENDENT MOVING COMPANIES

Some of the best moving companies are the local independent companies. Often these companies are family owned, and you can talk to one of the owners personally.

Value is where the best quality meets a fair price. Local independents do not have the overhead that the van lines do. They may not be as competitive on cross country moves because they lack the van lines national network. For local and regional moves, independents can't be beat!

Independents prefer itemized quotes but do hourly moves as well. They do not need to price in pounds because only your belongings will be on the moving truck. It is a distinct advantage to have exclusive use of the moving truck during your move.

Moving quotes can be obtained online or over the phone, but the most preferred method is an in-home estimate. Quality independents normally have a written guarantee in addition to the standard contract. It is difficult to compare quotes from budget/apt. movers because of the quality/price gradient.

Experienced movers like to work for the van lines or the local independents. No moving crew wants to be on an under booked job. The best crews get paid based on what they actually accomplish and are responsible for their own damages. The most careful crew is a responsible crew that is paid fairly.

Good movers, the same as their customers, don't like to argue over the move price on move day. Upfront pricing is the mark of the quality moving company. The "bait and switch" is the tactic of the "low baller" moving company.

Reputation is very important for quality independent moving companies. They do not have the corporate, military, or general government contracts and mainly move people that are actually paying for their own moves. While prices are competitive for the same moving services, quality is the main selling point for the local independent moving company.

Check out the reputation of the companies you are considering. Watch video reviews, ask family and friends if they had heard any feedback about the companies and find a moving company you would be happy to recommend to those you care about.

STORAGE CONTAINERS AND TRUCKS BY THE FOOT

PODS and other companies that offer portable storage containers have given people another option in moving and storage. People contact the company, set up a date, and they deliver the storage container on one day and pick up the container on another day.

The standard size is 16 feet. If you need storage, this could be a great option. Just like regular self-storage units, PODS often have deals, discounts, and coupons.

People often hire movers to load their storage container(s). Here are a few problems I have seen folks run into. Take note, learn from someone else's mistakes. Find out what the cost is for additional storage containers at the last minute. People are notorious for underestimating how much storage space they will need. If you get a 16-foot container, it is not the same as a sixteen feet worth of moving truck space. Storage containers are not as wide and they're shorter. (Unless you are using shipping containers.)

Get the storage container delivered ahead of time. Don't let an unexpected delay put a crimp in your moving plans.

Make sure you have rented plenty of pads to protect your belongings. In addition to the to the road vibration of transit, the containers will be moved around with a forklift at the warehouse. People think because it is a storage container they will need less blankets when in reality, they should pad their furniture the same as if they were loading a moving truck. If your furniture is not secure and padded, it will be damaged.

Compare the cost of the total move. Hiring movers to load and unload your storage container, plus the cost of the container itself, pad rental, and storage adds up. Sometimes it's more cost effective to just have a professional moving company take care of it all. There is less hassle with a turnkey operation, and insurance is included. With storage units and storage containers alike, you are "self-insured." You are responsible.

Some freight companies will drop off a semi-trailer at your house. You have a predetermined time to load the semi-trailer. The trailer is picked up by the freight company, driven to your new place, and dropped off once again for you to unload. The network of drivers and logistical specialists help make this cost effective, especially for long distance moves. If you ever saw an ABF Truck pulling three semi-trailers, you have seen "Truck by the foot" in action. Sometimes it takes longer to get your stuff from point A to point B because you are on their schedule.

You are responsible for damages and need to provide your own packing blankets, same as if you rented a truck. People often hire a professional moving company to provide skilled labor to both load and unload the semi-trailer.

Professional movers bring their own dollies when they are hired to load and unload your truck. You provide all the moving blankets and moving straps. It is just like hiring a crew to load and unload your U-HAUL. With a rental truck, you save the big bucks by driving the long haul yourself. "Truck by the foot" outsources hours behind the wheel. This is a welcome variation of the DIY truck rental.

INTERNET COMPANIES

The internet is a popular place to find a moving company. On the web, a small start-up can look just as impressive as the national van lines. Don't let the skills of a talented web designer give you a false sense of security. If you are going to trust a company to send men into your home, take the time to research the company.

Licensed, bonded, insured, and members of the BBB are the basics. Most reputable moving companies will also be members of a trade association for the household goods moving industry; Southwest Movers Association (SMA) and American Movers and Storage Association (AMSA).

Membership in the local Chamber of Commerce shows a commitment to the local community. All this research can be done online from the convenience of your laptop while you drink your morning coffee.

The internet has a lot of information, both truth and propaganda. There are lots of websites that will let you write and read reviews of companies. Some, however, are biased: asking companies to pay to have bad reviews buried and good reviews promoted. Take written internet reviews with a grain of salt. Unhappy customers make more noise than those who are satisfied.

Fake reviews are in abundance, competitors trying to make some company look bad, and companies writing positive reviews about themselves under ten different pseudonyms. Is a slick salesman that has sent you links to negative internet information about a competitor being helpful, or showing you his handy work? A new company will have a small digital footprint. A company that has been around seventeen years will have a larger digital footprint, both good and bad. You can't please everyone, not in the moving business.

I like video reviews because they're much harder to fake. Some companies clear their record by changing their name. If you are dealing with a new company, that should be a consideration. Is it an industrious start up or a sleazy outfit pressing the reset button?

Some of the most impressive moving company websites that I've seen are not moving companies at all. Brokers and lead generation companies are not actual moving companies. They do not employ any actual moving crews. These companies live online and provide a very professional interface to the "customer".

Lead generators take your information and sell it to moving companies. Brokers book your move, take payment online, then outsource your move to an actual moving company. The quality of your moving experience is based on the crew that shows up on move day. Why add a middle man and unknown variables?

I recommend using the movers your friends trust. If you are seeking a mover without a referral, then do the basics. Research the moving company: licensed, bonded, insured, testimonials, video reviews, and a good BBB record. Just getting an in-home estimate gets you a higher class moving company. Brokers and lead generators do not come to your house; they're probably not even in the same state.

You can learn a lot about a moving company on line, but how much more can you learn in a face to face interview, after the in-home estimator has inventoried and prepared a moving quote in your home for you upcoming move.

CHAPTER FIVE
THE ART OF PACKING BOXES

Packing up the house is a substantial portion of the cost of a typical home move. Many people opt to pack boxes themselves to save money. Packing yourself makes sense because what is normally needed for a professional move are not required to pack up a home, i.e. moving truck, dollies, and strong men.

Packing boxes is a skill set, the same as moving furniture, but no heavy lifting is required. Moving the contents of a house is normally set in a tight time frame (between house closings); whereas, packing the house can be started early and done at your convenience.

If you do decide to pack yourself, there are techniques and methods to insure success. Make sure to use the right size box for the job. Use plenty of packing paper and bubble wrap for breakable items. Always seal your boxes with tape. Never fold the flaps or leave boxes open. Boxes sealed with tape are structurally stronger and less likely to collapse in on themselves on move day when they are stacked on a dolly and rolled out to the moving truck.

Packing is an art form. When you purchase a new item, it comes in its own box with custom packaging made just for it. When you are packing your house, everything is packed in standard boxes with multipurpose packing paper and bubble wrap. Most people do not save all the original boxes and custom packaging from all their purchases, and that's okay.

People ask, "what all needs to be packed?" A rule of thumb is, if it can fit in a box, pack it in a box. If the item is less than twenty-four inches, it needs to be packed in a box. On move day, there should only be furniture and sealed boxes for the moving crew to take care of. It should be noted that most moving companies will not move open, unsealed boxes.

Do not over fill a box. Pack books and heavy items in smaller boxes (1.5 cu. ft.). Pack lighter items like clothes and toys in larger boxes (3.1 cu. ft.). Try to keep packed boxes under forty pounds. Over size/weight boxes cost more to move.

There are some items you must pack and move yourself: guns, ammunition, chemicals, propane tanks, drugs, jewelry, cash, gold, pets, and kids. If it is exceptionally valuable, move it yourself. If it is dangerous or could damage items in the truck, move it yourself. If it could start a fire, move it yourself. If you have prescription drugs, insulin, et cetera, move it yourself.

Make sure to label your packed boxes, both the contents, as well as, where you want it placed at the new home.

The right supplies will make the job easier. Make sure all packing is done before your move date. Nothing causes more confusion than trying to pack a house while it's being moved.

PRIORITY BOXES AND SPECIALTY ITEMS

It takes time to pack up a house. It sometimes takes longer to unpack. It is a good idea to label some "priority boxes" that you will need the first night in your new home. Second day items you will need, as well as first week items should also be noted.

I have seen new mothers frantically open boxes left and right looking for baby formula and diapers. There are things you will need to unpack on the first night to get settled in. Plan ahead and save yourself some stress later.

Common items are: toothbrush/paste, toilet paper, prescription medicine, personal hygiene, baby supplies, pet food, coffee maker/cups, pajamas, and a fresh change of clothing. Whatever you know you will need to unpack first, label it. Make your life a little easier by planning ahead.

Specialty items sometimes require specialty packaging and oversized boxes. Sometimes crating is needed when a cardboard box just will not do.

Note, if you have anything that requires a specialty box, notify your moving company. The in-home estimate is the best time to go over items that require special consideration.

Chandeliers and eight-foot sailfish, normally need to be crated. Most specialty items can be packed in an oversized triple corrugated box. All crating/packaging needs to be completed before your move day.

HOME OFFICE AND LIBRARY

Packing up the home office is fairly simple because there are mainly bulky items and paper products. The more glass and breakables, the longer a room takes to pack.

It is important to empty the desk drawers and file cabinets. Some moving companies will let you leave metal file cabinets full, but lateral file cabinets must always be emptied. The ball bearings in the track can break loose if stressed. Tipping a loaded file cabinet on a moving dolly is enough stress to damage the filing cabinet track.

Files can easily be transferred to a file/book box and kept in order with proper notation.

Labeling the contents of each box will make life easier later on. When packing a house always consider the fact that you will be unpacking the house as well.

Office supplies and equipment should be rolled in packing paper: pens, paper clips, staplers, tape dispensers, et cetera.

If you have the original boxes for the office computers, monitors, and printers, use them. If not, wrapping them in bubble wrap and placing them in a size appropriate box with packing paper will work just fine. Label them "fragile."

Computer towers are often moved as a standalone, wrapped

with a moving blanket on move day. Ask your moving company if this service is offered. All wires and cables should be packed in boxes. Pay special attention to your printer's toner, and ink cartridges, they can sometimes leak or spill out and get all over everything. It is recommended to remove toner and ink cartridges and wrap them in a plastic bag.

All bookshelves must be emptied, and books packed. Pack books flat as not to stress the binding.

Plaques, awards, models, and miscellaneous knick knacks should be wrapped with packing paper and bubble wrap.

The office is often the easiest room to pack due to its organized nature. 1.5 cu. ft. book boxes are the most common box for the library and office because books and files make up the bulk of these rooms.

LIVING ROOM AND GAME ROOM

Living rooms are relatively easy to pack. Sofa, love seat, coffee table, end tables, and television do not require any packing to begin with. The entertainment center must be emptied, and contents packed. Lamps, pictures, and knick knacks, et cetera, must be packed as well.

All the toys and games in the game room must be boxed. Books that are on shelves, video games, and photo albums must be packed as well.

Pictures and wall decor must be boxed before the movers arrive. Although, some movers will move large (over eighteen inches)

pictures and mirrors by wrapping them in a moving pad on move day. While this can save a great deal of money on large picture/mirror boxes, the proper way is to box each large picture/mirror into a picture box.

Small pictures (less than eighteen inches) can be packed back to back in a 3.1 cu. ft. box. Make sure to wrap them with plenty of packing paper or bubble wrap.

Box small lamps and lamp shades separately.

Box up the DVD player, DVR, video game console, and other components by wrapping with bubble wrap and packing paper.

Books, photo albums, DVD's and CD's should be packed in 1.5 cu. ft. book boxes.

Wrap breakable decor and knick knacks with extra care.

Games and toys seldom require packing paper or bubble wrap.

All in all, the living room is fairly straightforward when it comes to packing

THE BEDROOMS

It's always a good idea to pack a fresh set of sheets in one of your priority boxes. Making up your beds is one of the last things you will be doing on move day. Don't waste time

searching through countless boxes for fresh linens. This is especially true if you have children. Putting baby to sleep is one of the big accomplishments of the first day in your new home.

Packing up a bedroom is fairly easy. Clothes are placed in large boxes and require no bubble wrap or any extra packing care. The only danger your clothes face is from an accidental bleach spill or getting wrinkled.

All hanging clothes should be packed in a wardrobe box. Install the metal rod and hang your clothes up.

Folded clothes should be packed in a 3.1 cu. ft. box.

Dress shoes should be wrapped in packing paper, unless you have the original shoe box they came in. I have always been surprised at how many people hold onto their old shoe boxes.

Most moving companies will let you leave clothes in your dressers and chest of drawers, but armoires and hi-boys must be emptied before your move.

You must pack all papers, letters, photographs, perfume, and makeup bottles. Only fabric can remain in a dresser or chest of drawers. Check with your moving company because some companies require that everything is emptied.

All boxes should be labeled with which bedroom it came from and sealed with tape. Bedrooms are easy to pack.

THE BATHROOMS

Bathrooms are the easiest rooms in the house to pack, due to their small size. The main concern with the bathrooms is mixing up little items and the contents of the containers spilling out. Some of your bathroom items should already be packed in your priority box, and labeled for immediate use at your new home.

Towels and toilet paper can be packed in 3.1 cu. ft. boxes.

Wrap small items in packing paper to prevent them from getting mixed up. For example, Bobbie pins can be wrapped and taped to keep them together.

Make sure all lids are on securely. If you have a product that could spill out or leak, put it in a zip lock bag.

Cleaning supplies need extra care. If the lid does not seal tight it is better to throw it out than for it to spill on your clothes boxes. Wrap all glass bottles with paper, and keep all containers upright.

Label each box with "This side up," with an arrow. The boxes should be sealed with tape and labeled which bathroom it goes in at the new house.

KITCHEN AND DINING ROOM

Packing the kitchen is generally the most time consuming and requires the greatest skill. Glass cracks and

breaks quite easily, so here are some techniques the professionals utilize to avoid damages.

The novice packer almost never uses enough packing paper. As with all packing, make sure the box is full and nothing can rattle or roll. Even if you have to fill half the box with crinkled packing paper, make sure the box is full. A box that is partially full is inherently weaker and could collapse in on itself. The contents of half full boxes will bounce around and cause breakage.

The best packing advice is to wrap everything with plenty of packing paper, and to pack tightly all the way to the top of the box. Seal the box with tape, and label the contents.

3.1 cu. ft. boxes can be used for pots, pans, and small appliances. Use 1.5 cu. ft. boxes and dish packs for all breakables.

Stemware should be rolled in a sheet of packing paper and packed vertically. Do not pack glass on its side. Glass is much stronger on its end. Wrap each piece of glassware with a full sheet of paper.

Plates should be well wrapped and packed on end.

Silverware and utensils should be wrapped in paper bundles and taped to prevent movement.

Knives should be wrapped in paper, taped, and then rolled in a piece of cardboard. Crinkled paper should be placed in the sharp end of the knife pack.

Sharp knives that are improperly packed can cut through the box and injure someone. I have seen sharp knives sticking out of boxes, and yes, good men have sustained injuries. You just don't expect a dagger jutting out the side of a moving box.

The contents of the fridge should be packed in a cooler. The fridge must be emptied before it is moved. This is a good time to clean out your fridge and throw out what you don't want anymore. The coolers can be the last items loaded on the truck and the first to come off.

Being that the kitchen is the hardest room to pack up in a typical home, people often request a partial pack job. You can hire the professional packers to box up just your kitchen if you choose.

PANTRY AND LAUNDRY ROOM

Pantries are the easiest to pack. It is just like grocery shopping, but in reverse. Instead of "paper or plastic," you have cardboard boxes. Instead of lugging bags from the car, you have the movers roll your boxes on dollies.

Pack the bottles and canned goods in 1.5 cu. ft. boxes.

Pack the light items in 3.1 cu. ft. boxes, i.e. cereal, pasta, soup, et cetera.

This is a good time to go through your stocks and donate items you no longer want or need. Never pay to move something you are planning to throw out or give to charity.

Laundry rooms have special considerations. I was once on a move where we were hired to unload a customer's U-HAUL, their route took them over a mountain pass. The altitude change caused a pressure change in a bottle of bleach. The bleach leaked out of its box and onto the box below it. Their suits and evening dresses were in this particular wardrobe box. An 88-cent bottle of bleach caused thousands of dollars' worth of damage. Throw out cleaning supplies that

could damage your sofa or wardrobes if accidently spilled.

All containers should be packed upright and lids secure. Label these boxes with "this side up," an arrow, and seal all boxes with tape.

THE GARAGE

Garages have their own challenges, unique to each individual. Some people's garages are very organized, everything is already in a rubber maid tubs. On the other hand, some garages look like a storage unit for the Beverly Hillbillies. Most people fall somewhere in the middle.

The best time to clean out your garage and attic is before your move. Don't pay to move something you were going to throw out. Have a garage sale before move day, and pick up some extra cash. You can also lighten your load by giving to a charity of your choice. Lots of charities will pick up donations or have convenient drop off locations. Some moving companies will haul off items to their charity as a service to their community at no charge to you. Ask for details, each moving company has their own policy.

Pack garage items in strong boxes. Dish packs make a good choice. Long handled tools can be bundled and shrink wrapped together.

Please empty the fuel out of your power tools. Moving companies cannot move anything flammable or explosive, i.e., gas cans, paints, pesticides, or any other dangerous chemicals. This is a state law. Moving companies have a "household goods" license, not a "hazard" or "flammable" endorsement.

This is a good thing. You don't want chemicals or flammable gas in the same truck as your furniture, clothes, and family photographs. That is how trucks catch on fire.

The garage makes a great staging area to stack boxes to get them out of your way. As always, label the contents of each box and what room you want it to be placed in at the new house. Make sure each box is sealed with tape.

A well packed house helps make the actual move day go smoothly. Boxes marked with contents and location (room name), simplify unpacking. Most folks unpack themselves, even if they did hire professional packers.

Unpacking is the other side of this equation. Help balance that equation with the right pack job.

CHAPTER SIX
BEFORE MOVE DAY

Moving is stressful. Some rank it on the same list as death, divorce, and bankruptcy. But unlike accidents, betrayal, and the economy crashing. Household relocations can be well planned, well organized, and well prepared for.

What is easy for the expert is hard for the novice. With a little knowledge and planning, your move can go smoothly. You can know what pitfalls to avoid, what questions to ask, and what to expect on move day.

You have your new place and a move date, but there are a lot of things you still have to consider. If you have bought or are building your dream house, you have probably dealt with a mountain of paper work that you did not even know existed before. The home buying experience is complex and a large book on its own.

Money is always a consideration. Nobody wants to over pay. Everybody wants the best value for their dollar. Unfortunately, not everyone is willing to do their research and acquire much needed knowledge. It is all too easy to skimp on the move when money is tight. Buying a house is expensive. Buying furniture to fill the house is expensive too. People often use moving to a new place as a reason to redecorate and add new furnishings.

Hiring a mover is a means to an end. You are paying for men, moving boxes, and a truck, but the goal is simple; Move all my stuff from point A to point B. You are really paying for a service, an experience. By definition, an experience that is better the less you notice it and the faster that it is over with.

Depending on money, friends, family, and time, you may be moving yourself, or DIY. Maybe you are planning a hybrid move, using a mover for the big things and moving the rest yourself, or perhaps you are using a professional moving company to handle everything. A full service move.

Renting a moving truck can be simple and convenient. Hiring a professional moving company can be done with a phone call and an in-home estimate. Understanding the companies and the right questions to ask can make all the difference in your moving experience.

You have four options to consider. Find out what suits you and your pocketbook best.

1. Pack all the boxes and move everything yourself. DIY.
2. Pack all the boxes and move all the small stuff yourself. Have a professional moving company move all the big items.
3. Pack all the boxes yourself. Hire a professional moving company to move all your furniture and sealed boxes. No rental truck or rental dollies needed. Most people choose this option. You can save a lot of money packing yourself.
4. Hire a full-service move. The movers will pack your boxes, and move everything. This is the stress-free option.

PREMOVE LOGISTICS

Nothing can sabotage your moving experience like poor planning. Whether you hire a full service moving company or are renting a moving truck, there is still a ton of stuff to consider that has nothing to do with the actual move. Moving all your personal belongings from point A to point B is only one aspect of your relocation.

Kids need to be withdrawn from their old school and enrolled in their new school. Parents will often move for the sole purpose of having their children go to a better school district.

Utilities need to be transferred. Water, electric, internet, and gas need to be shut off at the old address and turned on at your new home. It is a good idea to have your utilities overlap by a few days. The phone numbers to all of your

utilities should be saved on your phone or written down. (In the appendix, there is a place to save your helpful numbers.)

I have been on moves where the electric company had already shut off the lights and we were moving with lanterns and flash lights. This happens more than you would think with folks that try to cut corners. One person set the cutoff the day after their move, only to have their house closing delayed.

Another person said, "I told them to cut it off at 5 PM," and the electric company cut the power first thing in the morning. Pay for a few extra days and avoid the stress. Good lighting and AC is key to a successful move, and no one wants to spend the first night at their new home without water, AC, heat, the lights on, or the coffee maker working.

If you are renting a rental truck, it should be booked three weeks ahead of time. Rent it for a few extra days. You can always return it early. The cost is much less expensive three weeks before your move. If you need extra days with your rental truck at the last minute, you will pay a premium. If all the rental trucks are rented out at the end of the month, and you need to keep your truck for a few extra days, that puts the rental company in a bind. Your truck is already rented to another customer.

If you are hiring a professional, you should get at least three moving quotes from reputable moving companies. You should try to reserve your move date three weeks ahead of time. If your move date changes, notify your mover as soon as possible. The moving industry is a logistics industry. Professional moving companies will bend over backwards to accommodate your moving date. Priority is always given to customers that have already reserved their date.

One customer had their closing delayed by the title company. The paperwork was missing some small thing. We were already booked up for the end of the month. We had been turning away business for the last week. (There are always folks that think that they can call today for a move tomorrow at the end of the month. Quality movers do not overbook and fill all their time slots well ahead of time.) Because this was our customer, we accommodated their move date change, even though we were already booked up at the end of the month. We worked until one in the morning, but we got the move done and got our customer out of a jam. Moving companies give priority to those already on their schedule.

Plan for a babysitter on move day. You do not want small children around the house during the move. Heavy furniture being carried out of the house and children do not mix. The movers will be concerned with not bumping into your kids, when all of their attention should be focused on the task at hand: moving furniture without damaging it.

Find a pet sitter for move day. Pets under foot cause problems. I have also noticed that dogs get stressed out with strangers moving everything out of the house. This happens more than you would think, the dog will be tied up or in a cage, or in some cases loose in the home. The dog barks at the movers as they are moving out all the boxes and furniture. The dog looks at its owner, then at the moving men, then back to the owner, and barks. The dog can't understand what is going on. The house that the dog has sworn to protect is being emptied by strangers, and the owner won't do anything about it. "What's wrong with my owner, they are taking everything," the dog seems to be saying. At the new house, the dogs are normally as happy as can be, as all your personal belongings come pouring into your new home. Save your dog the stress, find a pet sitter.

Planning before your move is the first step in having a smooth moving experience. Organize, make lists, and set up a schedule.

PREPARING FOR YOUR MOVE DAY

Packing everything in boxes is the major part of preparing for move day. There are other things to consider when preparing your home for move day. Some things are obvious, other suggestions may seem counterintuitive.

You should refrain from watering your house plants three days before your move. Some people do just the opposite. Thinking that they are helping their plants by watering them right before the stress of moving. What they are really doing is causing a slipping hazard in the moving truck and causing water, dirty plant water, to get on their boxes and furniture.

Water your plants at the new house. Also after the move you should prune your plants. That will invigorate growth and help them come back after the stress of the move.

BBQ grills need to be cleaned before move day. I once picked up a grill and the grease trap spilled all over my pant leg. The reason to clean the grill and remove the grease is to protect all your other furniture. We do not want grease or soot on the truck floor or moving blankets. It will track on everything else.

Moving is a great time for spring cleaning. Anything that you are planning to donate to charity should be done before the move. Any crating should be done before the move, along with the packing. Any specialty items should be addressed and planned for before the move. Items that movers cannot move or you would prefer to move yourself, should be cleared before move day or in a designated pile marked "Do not move".

All boxes should be sealed with tape and marked what room they will go in at your new home. Boxes should be kept under forty pounds, if possible.

Most of move preparation is common sense. Making sure you are ready move day, makes the moving experience that much easier to deal with.

PREPARING YOUR NEW HOME

Your new place should be ready, shouldn't it? The place is empty, all you need to do is move your boxes and furniture into the right rooms. Right? Here are some considerations.

The walkway, the carpeting, and the hard floors are all factors in your move. Are you going to lay down plastic to protect the carpet? Is the moving company going to lay down carpet protectors? If so what is the additional cost? Is it included in the quote? Professional movers normally have door protectors, and door jamb covers.

Hardwood floors and linoleum can be damaged quite easily by faulty skids or wheels. I have seen fridges tear gaping holes in linoleum floors. Dressers, sofas, chairs, and anything with feet has the potential to damage a floor. You must be vigilant to check your casters, skids and wheels for defects. Often if the plastic protector is damaged the nail that held it in place is still jutting out. Just waiting to destroy your floor.

Floor damage can happen when you move furniture from a carpeted room to a hardwood floor room. In a carpeted room you have no idea of the potential damage a bad caster can cause. Carpet does not scratch.

I once moved a very large armoire from a carpeted bedroom to a bedroom with a wood floor. I told the wife that the casters needed to be replaced. I put the piece exactly where she wanted so they would not have to move it until it was fixed. As the crew continued to unload the truck, the husband decided to move the armoire to another wall by pushing it. His wife had not told him, and she was now taking care of the baby. The poor man put a three-foot scratch in his brand-new wood floor. This is also why professional movers pick up or dolly furniture, sliding furniture is frowned upon.

The walkway must be clean. Sometimes new houses have mud on the walkway because of the new sod. Before your move make sure your walkway will be clean. The moving truck is clean, your new home is clean, should not your walkway be clean as well? Mud on the walkway will get tracked in to the house and the moving truck. Movers cannot take their shoes off because of safety reasons, as well as being impractical.

I once had a customer ask for us to remove our shoes while we were carrying a piano. Movers have broken bones by accidently dropping something heavy on their toes even with their shoes on. They are not going to take their shoes off. Moving heavy furniture is inherently risky, and not to be done barefoot.

The best way to prepare your new home for the movers is to know where everything is going. Don't make the movers stand there holding a piece of heavy furniture while you discuss with your spouse where the piece of furniture is going to end up. Have a plan before the move day. An organized move is a smooth move.

PLANNING FOR THE UNEXPECTED

The thing about the unexpected is, you don't expect it. A lot can go wrong with a move. Closings are suddenly delayed for often the simplest reasons. Every week we have to reschedule move dates because of closings being bumped. Not such a big deal unless it happens at the last minute, or if the folks you sold your home to need you out, but you have no home to move to. It's all because of some paperwork glitch at the title company. It is always a good idea to have a backup plan and a flexible moving company.

Professional moving companies offer last minute storage options. Ask about storage, even if you have no intention of needing it. Sometimes if you are delayed by a day, you can store your furniture on the truck and avoid the cost of everything being moved twice. You will pay a storage on the truck charge.

Know where the water cut off is at your old house as well as your new home. Disconnecting washing machines can reveal problems that you did not know existed. If you can't shut off the water at the washing machine, you can't move the appliance. I have even seen brand-new homes with plumbing problems. Once when I was connecting a washer, the PVC connection twisted off. It had been seated incorrectly by the plumber. Water started pouring everywhere and our customer did not know where the water cut off was. We found the valve shut off and cut off the water supply. Don't expect your movers to have this skill set. Know how to shut off your own water supply.

Make a trip to Home Depot and pack up some extra skids/casters if you are moving to a home with hardwood floors. Just in case. If your washer hoses are old, now is the time to pick up a new set while you are at the hardware store. The same goes for your ice maker connections. Pick up a kit. You can always return it if you don't need it. Be prepared, consider all contingencies.

If you are moving yourself or just hiring a mover for the big stuff, what is your plan if your friends don't show up, bail, or flake? What is your backup plan? If you hired a mover for the big items, it may be easy enough to add some more items to your moving list. If you hired a "lowest cost mover" and they are a no show, what is the backup plan? Always give yourself options to prepare for the unforeseen.

The best plans are the ones made ahead of time

CHAPTER SEVEN
MOVE DAY

You have spent a month preparing for this day, you have the keys to your new home, your entire house is packed, all your boxes are labeled and sealed, the kids and the dog are with grandma, and you just got a call from the movers saying they were twenty minutes away. Enjoy your coffee because your day is off to a great start.

On move day, give yourself extra time. Plan for a "time cushion" that way if things take longer (and they always do), you are covered. You have planned for it. I was once on a job, packing the truck, when another moving crew arrived with a fully loaded truck. It turned out that the new residents from out of state were scheduled to move in at noon. Never plan a move out with a move in on the same day. The other movers and the new family sat there while we finished up. It's awkward and preventable.

Estimating move time is difficult. The quality and experience of your moving crew makes all the difference. If you have a "switchback" stair case, that will take longer than straight stair case. If there is a long walk, it will take more time then pulling the truck right up to the front door. Waiting for an elevator takes time. The kind of furniture that you have will affect how long the move takes for better or worse. Always plan for extra time on move

day. The "time cushion" reduces stress for everyone.

If your friends are helping, make sure that you know what they think is expected of them. Misunderstandings hurt friendships and cause problems on move day.

The foundation of preparation is what move day is built on. The quality and experience of the moving company can make all the difference. A quality moving crew can easily move an average house in one day.

Loading the Truck

Every piece of furniture must be wrapped and padded. Friends sometimes don't realize that just road vibration is enough for a cardboard box to ware through a dresser's finish on a 500-mile move. The pack job should be just as carefully done on a move across town as a move across the country. Ropes, straps, and blankets are the tools of the trade to prevent damage in transit. Glass tops and mirrors should be packed on

end, against the truck wall. Nothing should be able to move or slide around. If the item can't move and is wrapped in a moving blanket, it probably will not get damaged in transit.

If you hired a professional moving company, you don't have to worry about packing the truck. The professionals have you covered. The main thing you need to do to help the moving crew is to be there to answer any questions. Items

MAY need to be disassembled (e.g. fridge doors, large decks, oversized armoires and the like.) Some items WILL need to be disassembled, (washer/dryer, head boards/foot boards, bed frames, mirrors on dressers, and so on.)

Your in-home moving estimator would have covered these items with you and explained what was included in your quote.

If the movers disconnect your appliances for you (and quality moving companies do), check the water lines yourself. The water lines are the home owner's responsibility. A small leak in your ice maker hose or the washing machine connection could cause thousands of dollars of damage.

Loading the moving truck is a lot like playing Tetris. The crew will load furniture in the order that makes the most sense for packing the truck. Giving the crew a "tour" and saying which room is which, e.g. Emilie's room, the office, game room, and

so on, will make it easier at the unload.

Once the truck is loaded and the house is empty, do a walk through. Walk through the house with the movers and make sure nothing was left. Double checking now, can save grief later. You are responsible for giving the "all clear". If items are accidently left behind, that will be your responsibility.

Always do a final walkthrough.

THE DRIVE

Moving trucks drive slow. Experienced drivers try to reduce road vibration and road bumps. They will take turns slowly to minimize the centripetal force. This is a good thing, and if you are driving a rental truck, you would be wise to drive slowly as well.

Exchange cell phone numbers with the driver if you have not done so already. There are two options: to meet the moving crew at the drop off or have them follow you there. If they follow you, drive slowly.  Keep the moving truck in your review mirror. If you are meeting the crew at your new home, set up the time. It is common for the movers to get lunch on the way to the unload

I once had a customer want me to follow them, only to take off like a race car driver. I did not even try to keep up. I had my helper look up the drop off address and we proceeded. My cell phone rang. "Where are you guys?" I replied that I would just meet them at the drop off address. I am not going make a 26,000-pound fully loaded moving truck try and keep up with a 3000-pound sports car.

THE UNLOAD

Unloading a moving truck is faster and easier then loading the truck in the first place. When packing a moving truck, everything has to fit together and not get damaged. Every piece has to be wrapped and padded. Unloads are fairly straight forward and considered to be the downhill, to the loads uphill.

Of course, if there are stairs or long walks, this will add to the time. Location conditions always affect the time and effort of a moving job.

I was once on a move from a house with a thirty-six-inch front door to a home with a thirty-two-inch front door. It was an older house, built when doors were smaller. Items that sailed out of the old house now needed to be disassembled just to make it in the new home. Feet off the sofa and love seat, fridge doors had to be removed, and so on. Move conditions are always a factor.

The most important thing for you to do, is to direct the movers. Be right at the front door and direct traffic. At the beginning before a single box is unloaded give the movers a tour of your new home. This way when you say which room, they will know exactly what you are talking about. Show the movers where you want your furniture placed. It is much easier to place your furniture exactly where you want it while you have the man power, instead of waiting and trying to move things around yourself later.

Some pet peeves of professional movers at the unload: Customers that talk on the phone or text excessively, or are otherwise distracted as the truck is being unloaded. Standing there with a heavy load in your arms and your customer is not sure where they want it is another common problem. Customers that keep asking you to change the location of a piece of furniture. "That armoire I asked you to put in the

upstairs bedroom, well I now want it in the downstairs bedroom." Moving the same item over again is aggravating.

Being right there for your movers from the beginning and answering their questions will make the unload go faster and smoother, making everyone happy.

Double check the appliance connections. Any water leaks are the home owner's responsibility. Double check each room and make sure that everything is exactly where you want it. If you need an item moved, ask. Professional movers are normally happy to help. This may contradict with the "pet peeves," but this is your home, and everything needs to be perfect for you. Re-moving a couple items is no big deal. Asking for the movers to rearrange the house is.

Double check the moving truck. The driver has already double checked the truck but this way you have the peace of mind of seeing the empty truck for yourself. If setting up the beds and reattaching mirrors to dressers is part of the service or you have paid for this service, double check to make sure it was done. It is easy to overlook little things in the hustle and bustle of the unload when the end of a hard day is in sight.

Pay your movers. Cash, checks, and major credit cards are normally accepted by professional moving companies. Although, some companies only accept cash (a warning sign of a poor-quality company).

Ask ahead of time about payment options.

TIPPING THE CREW

If you are moving yourself and your friends are helping, then pizza and beer is all you need to provide. Of course, the understanding that you will at some point reciprocate is a form of soft payment.

If you have hired a moving company, the crew would appreciate a gratuity. The moving industry is a service industry. Just like you tip your waitress for good service, you should tip your movers for good service. Movers are held to a higher standard, though.

If your movers were unprofessional or they damaged stuff, call the company, and do not tip them. Tipping is a motivator in all service industries. The man/woman knows that if they do an exceptional job for their customer, they could receive a little extra. This is a great check and balance for quality service. In instances where the gratuity is already factored into the bill, the service worker gets paid the same regardless of performance, and it shows.

Moving companies do not factor in a gratuity. Paying cash directly to the movers is preferred, but you can add the tip to your check or credit card if it is more convenient for you.

How much should you tip? If you are not happy with the service, don't tip the movers at all, and report it to the moving company. If you are happy with the movers' service, it is entirely up to you. Consider what you would tip a waitress at Chili's. What percentage you would normally tip on the bill is a good number to consider splitting between the crew. If you tip twenty percent to the Chili's waitress, then split that between the crew, if you are moving long distance, you don't need to tip on the cost of the drive. Only tip for manual work performed, not mileage.

Of course, if the crew did an outstanding job for you, you may factor that into how much you want to tip them.

CHAPTER EIGHT
AFTER YOUR MOVE

Move day can be kind of hectic. Make sure your "priority boxes" are accessible, with all the items you are going to need first. If anything was damaged, note it on the move ticket and have the driver initial. If you notice damage later, you have a certain amount of time to make a damage claim by state law. The important thing now is to get settled in.

Organizing your new home can take some time. Hanging pictures, arranging decor, and getting everything just right. It is a good idea to look over all your furniture, make sure everything is in the same condition. You have time to make a damage claim, but it is a limited amount of time.

If you moved yourself and rented a truck, avoid fees, fill up the fuel tank, and clean out the box, and cab before you return it. Just leaving a Starbuck's coffee cup on the floorboard could cost you. Sweep out the truck yourself or the rental company will charge you for the service. Save some pictures of the rental truck after you return it, just in case. Check your credit card bill for overcharges. It is common for rental companies to charge you without notification. It is your responsibility to deal with charges that are in error. You probably will not know that there is a problem until the extra charges show up on your credit card statement.

Thank your friends. It is not uncommon to send thank you notes to those that helped you, and invite them to your house warming party for a nice meal. (This of course does not apply to the moving crew.)

Moving into a new house is the perfect time to organize and get everything just the way that you want it. It is also the time a lot of folks buy new furniture. The moving company that just moved you to your new home can often help you with the small jobs as well.

Double check that your utilities were shut off at the old house. Some people find out later, much later, that a utility service was not terminated as requested. There is a story about a cable provider that did not stop the service and ran up overdue charges. The person found out they were in collections when they tried to buy a car, and their credit score had fallen. The cable provider denied there was any request for termination of services. Of course, this person was put on hold by customer service for an hour to find out this information. They ended up paying for services that they never used and had requested canceled on move day. A form of extortion to save their credit score.

UNPACKING YOUR BOXES

Unpacking all your boxes can be as much work as it was to pack them in the first place. When you pack yourself, you save money, but you are also responsible for how well the contents were packed. Most moving companies will deny any claims for damage for boxes packed by a customer because "contents unknown."

If you hired a moving company to pack your boxes, they should be responsible for any damages. Always ask about their insurance and company policy. Professional packers, however, rarely have damage because they use so much packing paper.

Brake down all your used boxes so they are flat. All the old packing paper should be put into trash bags. Used moving boxes have value. You can store them in your attic for future use, or have them hauled away. Some movers will come and pick up your used boxes at no charge. If you have hired professional unpackers, they will haul off all the used boxes and packing paper as part of the service.

Unpacking is relatively stress free. There are no deadlines, and the move is already over. If the contents of the boxes were properly labeled, you can decide what to unpack first.

RATE YOUR MOVERS

Rate your moving experience. Some moving companies maintain an online testimonial board. Yelp, Angie's List, Google Reviews, and Yahoo are just a few places online to rate moving companies. People that take the time to rate the moving company, help expose the bad companies while highlighting the good moving companies.

Before you post bad reviews about your movers, give the moving company a chance to make it right. Posting bad comments online before contacting the company puts you in an adversarial position before you even begin to resolve your damage claim. You want a collaborative relationship as your damage claim is resolved.

Lots of moving companies rate their own movers and packers with customer feedback being a major factor. If a crew is getting bad feedback online, they may be fired. Local independent moving companies depend on customer feedback. Quality moving companies will protect their reputation.

If you have a great moving experience, please tell the company and post online to Yelp, Google reviews, and Angie's List. Just like bad movers deserve to be flagged, quality moving companies need good feedback. When people are happy with their moving experience, they often don't take the time to let others know. Quality movers get their business from referrals and reputation. Help them out.

DAMAGE CLAIMS

The industry standard is 60 cents per pound for damaged items; however, quality movers normally have an in-house policy to repair or replace what their movers damage within reason. These are questions to ask before you book your move.

If you purchased supplemental insurance, you will deal with an insurance adjuster. If you bought valuation you will be dealing with the moving company, same as if they have an "in-house policy". Again, each company is different. The range for legal movers is 60 cents per pound, all the way to repair and replace.

Unlicensed (illegal) movers may do whatever. Know what kind of company you are hiring before you hire them. A little research will make your moving experience that much better. Smooth moves do not happen by accident.

Any damage claims need to be made as soon as possible. Take pictures of the damage and email to the moving company along with a "statement of fact". Some quality moving companies have an online form that streamlines this process. You should get an acknowledgement within twenty days, but quality movers will acknowledge the same day.

Depending on the damage, a repair company may come out or a settlement offer will be made. Wood furniture almost always can be fixed by an experienced woodworker. Glass and mirrors can be custom cut. Some items are easier to replace or offer  a settlement. Examples include, TVs, dishes, and lamps.

If you and the moving company can't see eye to eye, what recourse do you have? Make a complaint with the local BBB and request arbitration. If the mover is a member in good standing with the BBB, they will be bound by the arbitration. Most quality movers will protect their BBB record, and they will try to avoid getting the BBB involved in the first place. The Department of Transportation offers mediation for licensed moving companies. You can make a complaint with DOT that will go on the company's record. Again, quality movers will take measures to protect their record with the state.

Quality moving companies know a damage claim is not the same as an unhappy customer. You can have something get damaged during your move and still be very happy with the service. A damage claim that is handled well can make you respect the moving company even more.

The important thing to remember is to avoid misunderstandings. Know what coverage you have and what the in-house policy is before you pick your moving company and reserve your move date.

A NEW MEMBER OF THE COMMUNITY

Settling in to your new house can take some time. Finding where everything is, meeting the neighbors, and getting your new home just the way you want it.

Most local Chamber of Commerce have a welcome pack, with helpful information about your new town. Discounts and coupons for local businesses exclusively for new residents. Even upcoming festivals and the town's history which would be fun for the kids.

Learning about the town's history and meeting local small business owners can help your family develop a sense of community as your family lays down roots of their own.

Small business owners are invested in the community with actions not words. Their long-term success is tied to the future of the community, so it would make sense that they understand their town and often sponsor events. If your daughter joins a soccer team, chances are a small business owner paid for her team's uniforms.

If you were happy with your moving company, save this information. People often need a mover to do small jobs. New houses sometimes need additional furniture, or new appliances.

One of the most common questions new neighbors have is, "How was the move?" followed with, "What moving company did you use?" People are always on the lookout for a good moving company. If your movers took care of you, take care of them with referrals.

Quality moving companies get most of their business from repeat customers and referrals.

CHAPTER NINE
DON'T BE A MOVING HORROR STORY

A lot can go wrong when you are moving to your new home. Most problems are small and can be easily overcome. But sometimes things go so bad it becomes a horror story. Some bad moving experiences can affect your entire life, not just your pocket book.

Doing your due diligence before you hire a mover and planning your move before move day will help you avoid most problems. There are circumstances that can come up that you may never have thought of. There are moving scams out there that you may never have heard of before. Crooks that prey on people when they are most vulnerable.

The news does "special reports" on moving scams every so often, but a search online and with the BBB will reveal the depth of the problem is far greater. There are bad companies that jack up your move price at the last minute with "add-ons," and then there are actual crooks that will hold your stuff hostage. There are bad workers that may be careless with your furniture, and then there are thieves that do the job as an opportunity to case out your new home.

I have heard a lot of, "I had a bad moving experience," stories over the years. They normally start out with, "I thought I had found the greatest deal." Sometimes folks get blinded with a low price.

People that think they can hire a moving crew with all the dollies and moving blankets, truck, and fuel for less than it would be to rent a truck and move themselves, are in for a surprise. People that think the $39 per hour ad on Craig's List is a good deal are not seeing the whole picture. A good deal is a move quote that is real. A good deal is being happy at the end of the move and paying what is expected.

Save yourself stress and hardship, or worse and hire a reputable moving company. Learn from other people's mistakes. Do your own research and plan your move accordingly. A smooth move is not an accident.

HOSTAGE LOADS

Just like auto shops can put a lean on your car and contractors can put a lean on your house for nonpayment of services rendered, moving companies can hold your stuff as collateral. State approved contracts normally state that you must pay for your move before the truck is unloaded. This is standard procedure. Failure to pay for your move could result is your stuff being hauled to storage at your expense. You could be charged for your move, the move to the company's storage warehouse, the move back to your house, and the costs of storage. If you refuse, you could forfeit your belongings and risk a judgement being filed against you in court.

Because this is a civil matter, you could take them to court, but the police will not help. If you call the police, they will say, "The movers have a signed contract, and this is a civil matter."

Quality moving companies have a reputation to protect. The "fly by nights" don't. The "name changes" could care less about BBB complaints. The "bait and switchers" could care less about internet reviews.

KHOU TV out of Houston did a report in 2001 about a clever moving scam. The bait, $39 per hour including shrink wrap, 2 men, the truck, everything. The ad was on Craig's List. The company name was a quality moving company with a BBB rating and a professional website linked to the Craig's List ad. The number, however, went to the crook's cell phone. On move day, two professional looking movers showed up on time from a different company. "The company that you booked with had a truck break down, we are covering the move for them. We normally do not do $39 hourlies, but we will honor the contract. Please sign here."

You are happy, before your mover told you they could not make it out, they got another moving company to cover your move. On time, fast, the right price. Well, it turns out that shrink wrapping is $90 per item, and they are wrapping everything. You are presented a much higher bill at the drop off. Payment is demanded in cash before the unload. The KHOU TV/BBB undercover investigations showed the scammers charge $900 just for shrink wrap on one move. It was in the contract: pay before unload and $90 per item to shrink wrap. Folks saw their $39.99 per hour move, jump to $1200, $1700, and $2300 according the news report.

Anyone can post a Craig's List ad and link it to a quality company. Call the moving company to ask a few questions about your move and confirm your move date. If they have never heard of you, you know you are about to be the victim of a scam.

Poor quality movers are notorious for dramatically increasing move prices on move day once all your stuff is already on their moving truck. Poor quality movers get a lot of business from internet brokers.

CBS news reported in 2015 that one in ten moves will report that their furniture was held hostage. The movers demanded more money.

Avoid scams, research the moving company. Avoid misunderstandings, review and understand what is included in your moving quote and move contract.

EXTENSIVE DAMAGE

An improperly packed truck can destroy your furniture. Inexperienced moving crews or crews that just don't care, can damage your furniture as they carry it out to the truck. People pay thousands of dollars for their furniture and then try to save a few dollars on their move. The experience of the moving crews is a metric some folks don't even think about when comparing prices.

I saw a commercial for Direct TV. They were showing movers destroying the family's furniture and their house. Dining table through the wall, the sound of glass breaking in boxes as they were slammed down on the floor, and mud being tracked in the house on white carpet. There were a several versions of the commercial with different kinds of destruction. I thought to myself, do movers have such a bad reputation, that Direct TV with all their high paid marketing teams have determined that the stereotype of the "mover" is the worst part of a move?

This is not what I see every day. I see professional men working hard providing quality service at competitive prices. I see boxes packed with care and moving trucks packed with skill. I see a professional company and crew make the hardest part of a family's relocation seem like the easiest part.

When people have an inexperienced crew or a crew that just does not care, things get damaged. If a company is hiding behind the government mandated 60 cents per pound, what does that really say about their service? What is worse than a company using the 60 cents per pound shield? The illegal movers that, after damaging your stuff and getting paid in cash, disappear. If you hire a "Chuck and a Truck" from an internet ad, what do you expect?

Almost every horror story I have heard about extensive damage, starts with a too good to be true low price and ends with the customer finding out after the fact that the moving company had a bad reputation, or worse yet, no reputation. Research the moving company before you hire them.

Everyone knows that you can't make everyone happy. Any mover that has been in business long enough will have some complaints.

Come with me on a little thought experiment. Imagine you are considering two moving companies. The first one has three complaints with the BBB. The second has six complaints with the BBB. Company one seems the obvious choice, right? Maybe not. What if company one has been in business for one year and has only one crew. While company two has been in business seventeen years and runs ten crews. That is a horse of a different color, now, isn't it?

Always compare complaint ratio to company size. Do not let the Name Changers fool you. Movers will "clear" their BBB record with a name change.

If you want to predict the quality of your moving crew, look at the company's guarantee. If it is their policy to repair or replace what their movers damage, well then, they have faith in their crews. If they hide behind 60 cents per pound, they expect that their movers will damage your furniture and drop your boxes. Only quality moving crews could let a company make such a guarantee.

ACCIDENT AND FIRE DAMAGE

If the truck is in an accident or catches on fire, the insurance company will get involved. You will make a claim, and you or the moving company will pay the deductible. Cargo insurance covers the contents of what is in the truck, but what if the movers do not have cargo insurance?

Some moving companies sub out their jobs to movers that own their own pickup trucks. The drivers pull the company's cargo trailer. The driver's liability insurance makes the pickup legal, (but not really unless the driver is paying for commercial insurance). What is missing is the cargo insurance. No cargo insurance and all your personal belongings are vulnerable in transit.

If you are renting a truck, you should make sure you buy the additional cargo insurance from the rental company, or consult your own insurance company. Sometimes your home owner's policy can add coverage for the move.

I have heard a story from another company. A helper was smoking by the truck, and dropped his cigarette on the moving blankets by accident. The entire truck caught on fire. It was a total loss. That is why moving companies have a strict "NO SMOKING" policy.

I had a friend that was involved in an accident, and the truck flipped over. Thank God that he and his helper were only bumped and bruised. The furniture however took a beating, but there was far less damage then you would expect. On account of the truck being packed and padded so tightly. The insurance company got involved and covered the damage. In this case, the company paid the deductible. The customer was inconvenienced but compensated.

Without cargo insurance, you the customers are out. A low-priced move from a cut-rate company or a "chuck and a truck" could be the most expensive move you ever make.

WHO ARE YOU LETTING IN YOUR HOUSE?

I don't really want to write about this. It has nothing to do with moving furniture, but as a father, I feel it needs to be said. This applies to all companies that send men into your home to perform their services or sell their goods. What do you know about the strangers you have invited into your home?

There was a story about a woman who was raped by a vacuum cleaner salesman. The story turned into a political football. At the center of it, the debate of whether a company should be held responsible for the actions of their independent contractors.

A detailed search will reveal that many home service industries have a black eye when it comes to poor quality workers with nefarious intentions. Whether you have had cable installed, a subcontractor doing a remodel, a plumber fixing the sink or a moving company helping you relocate; the quality of the crew is important.

Companies that do background checks are good, but that is really just the start. Criminals have to be "convicted" to have a criminal record. Checking references, history, coworker feedback, and just getting to know someone's character, are all part of finding men that will accurately represent the company.

You want men with a strong moral compass. It stands to reason if you hire a shady outfit, they are more likely to have shady characters working for them. If you hire a company with a reputation for quality service and fair prices, the people that work there will share the company culture.

The lowest price is seldom the best deal. Value is where the quality of service and the best price intersect. If you are not comparing companies that are licensed, bonded, insured, and have top quality moving crews, what are you actually comparing?

THE STOLEN MOVING TRUCK

If you are moving yourself, keep an eye on the moving truck. Crooks sometimes target rental trucks. Many a family has woken up from a good night's sleep at their hotel, only to find that their rental truck is gone. Now they are stranded in the middle of nowhere. Halfway to their new home with nothing.

Rental trucks can be attractive to thieves. They normally don't have an alarm system, and they are already loaded with an entire household worth of goods. Why break into a house and load a truck, when you can just steal a fully loaded moving truck? The roadside inns have the U-Hauls, Budgets, and Penskis clearly marked for the crook's convenience.

Ask about insurance when you rent the truck in the first place. I recommend staying at a better class hotel with security cameras. Park in front of the cameras and install a wheel lock. A steering wheel lock can be purchased for less than forty dollars. As always, keep the doors locked as well.

Take care when selecting a padlock for the back door of your rental truck. This is not the place to save money. Some locks are much harder to defeat then others. If standard bolt cutters can chop off your padlock, buy a better lock. All self-respecting thieves have a set of bolt cutters.

Moving companies have to deal with crooks too. Good companies take the necessary precautions. Quality moving companies go beyond hardened locks and cargo insurance.

With the technology today, some moving companies have outfitted their fleet with GPS trackers. Being able to track your goods in real time takes a lot of the stress out of the moving experience.

Quality moving companies go hand in hand with quality moving trucks, equipment, and moving crews.

CHAPTER TEN
THE RICH HISTORY OF THE MOVING INDUSTRY

The moving industry was born because of and has grown in parallel with the unprecedented creation of wealth over the last 140 years. Technology increased crop production and the amount of men and women needed to produce it. More people were free to buy their food and housing, and work in other industries. More wealth was created, and by trading value for value, every hardworking American could increase their personal wealth.

The more things you buy, the more things you have. At some point, you need someone to help you move. With the explosion of the middle class, more and more folks needed help moving. Smart entrepreneurs are always looking to fill an unmet need. Find their niche.

The professional furniture mover started plying his trade around the late 1800s. Mainly with local moves. For long distance moves, ships and railcars were used. But with ships and railcars, everything had to be in a crate or a barrel, so it was more like freight services. With furniture movers, household goods are individually wrapped, padded, and loaded into the truck/wagon.

The moving company got its start with the middle class. The poor did not have enough stuff to need movers (or the money), and the rich had servants or men that already worked for them to do the heavy lifting, but times have changed.

Today the rich, the poor, companies, and governments all use professional moving companies. The unique skill set, specialized equipment, and moving trucks make it a smart choice to hire men and women that know how to pack a box of china without it getting broken and how to pack a semi with furniture without any damage.

Today, even the poor have wealth that could not have been bought with a king's gold throughout history. A flat screen

TV, a ton of electronics, mattresses, fridges, washing machines, and clothes dryers. The personal belongings of a poor American bests yesterday's nobility. Technology and hardworking Americans have made everybody's lives better and increased everybody's wealth. Professional moving companies are here to help you move all of it.

The moving industry has grown with the population and the economy. As a service business, it cannot be outsourced to another country like so many of our manufacturing jobs have been.

Moving is hard work. To be a mover, you need a good work ethic and be able to perform hard manual labor all day. It is not surprising that professional movers are physically strong and take pride in a job well done. There is a certain satisfaction in hard physical work that you have to do with your hands and can see immediate progress. When a house full of heavy furniture is emptied and packed into the moving truck without a damage, there is a certain satisfaction in the visible manifestation of the work that has been accomplished.

TEN THOUSAND YEARS OF DO IT YOUR SELF MOVERS

Human prehistory is rich with wandering peoples. Over thirteen thousand years ago the first Americans were walking over the land bridge with their stuff in tow. Of course, they did not call themselves Americans. Back then people moved themselves. No moving company needed.

With the invention of the wheel, folks could make carts, and that made moving a little easier. But still, folks moved themselves. Only kings and the super-rich had enough stuff to need movers, but they had slaves and subjects to do the heavy lifting for them.

It is interesting to note that when humans were hunters and gathers and moving around the most, they had the least amount of stuff. Packing up the whole tribe was no big deal.

Down came the tents, and they were off to follow the migration patterns of their prey.

Planet Earth was colonized this way. Year by year, generation by generation, and little by little, there were humans on six out of seven continents. That's not too shabby for walkers with backpacks.

As the agriculture revolution took hold, people moved less, staying close to their crops, and the upcoming harvest. Young men and women would get married, start a life together, and move to a place of their own. Normally still close by the tribe and the mother in law. The "local move" was born, but just like many newlyweds today, they just did not have enough stuff to hire a moving company. They were DIYers.

During the great conquests of the ancient empires, the winning army would often carry their loot back to their capitals, but back then the military was not yet outsourcing to moving companies. The army took care of it themselves. Probably for the better because professional moving companies do not move slaves and livestock and also recommend you move your old coins, jewelry, and gold yourself.

The DIY movers have a proud tradition dating back to time immemorial. For most of human history, folks moved themselves. Now they can rent a moving truck and DIY in style, or hire a moving company and enjoy the ease of a professional move.

GO WEST YOUNG MAN

The 1800s saw an unprecedented migration west. The covered wagon was the method of choice for most DIYers. Your wife, kids, and

everything you owned could easily fit in its spacious wooden box. Normally powered with two horse power, it could transverse rivers that were not flooded and were shallow. The wagon's strong axels could be replaced, if needed, in route. Just chop down an oak tree and shape to specifications.

There was no profit for moving companies with small jobs going long distances and nothing to haul back. About the only professional movers that made the covered wagon move west are the men that decided on a career change or fell in love with the farmer's daughter. Not surprisingly for families with love struck farmer's daughters and son-in-law movers, everything was wrapped, padded, and not even a tea cup was broken on their move out west.

Back in the big cities, horse drawn moving wagons were rolling down the street on local moves.

THE BIRTH OF AN INDUSTRY

With the technological advancement of the internal combustion engine and the steel frame, the moving truck was born. With better roads and gas-powered trucks, moving became more practical. The movers could drive to your house, load up all your furniture then drive to your new home, and unload your furniture just where you wanted it.

In some ways, not much has changed in principal since that first motorized truck. In other ways, the industry has been revolutionized. The need for movers has tracked the wealth of the nation. As people buy more stuff, they end up needing help to move it. As the population grew from tens of millions to hundreds of millions, the moving industry has kept pace with good companies providing quality service.

In 1919, Ward B. Hiner founded American Red Ball Transit. He thought moving goods from city to city in motorized trucks instead of by railroads would eliminate the need to crate furniture. Instead of loading on a truck, unloading at the rail car, then unloading into another truck (or wagon) at the new city, he could just drive to the new city. Red Ball was the first interstate carrier. The movers would load up at your house, and drive to your new home. A big improvement over crating everything for the railroads and moving everything four times (house to truck, truck to rail, rail to truck, and truck to new home).

Many companies followed his lead. Soon the trucking industry was a fierce competitor of the railroads. Ending a very old monopoly. One problem remained, after the unload an empty truck was on the road. There is no money in empty trucks.

In 1928, a group of moving companies formed an alliance to try and share moves to keep their trucks full. That marks the beginning of the van lines. They became known as Allied van lines. Some of the oldest moving companies that are still in business are United van lines and Mayflower van lines. They were moving companies before they both became van lines.

As the roads kept getting better and the trucks bigger, the moving industry continued to serve the growing American economy. The moving business has always been a service business

GOVERNMENT REGULATION

President Roosevelt introduced unprecedented regulation and new government programs in his effort to control the American economy in the wake of the great depression.

The motor carrier act was passed in 1935. Its purpose was to "regulate competitive practices and promote fair competition."

In 1948, congress passed the Reed-Bullwinkle act. This allowed companies to establish collective rates and full immunity from anti-trust laws. For a small moving company, it was difficult to meet the requirements and the van lines were the major players. Over regulation is an effective way to stop competition.

In 1980, congress deregulated the trucking industry. The number of licensed carriers jumped from a few hundred to more than twenty thousand in a short time. Movers now had to compete for your business. Prices fell, and for some companies, quality improved.

The range of prices, services, and kinds of moving companies were wide and varied. Things were not as simple as when there were just a few van lines (with collective rates) to choose from.

Suddenly folks that had always had to move themselves, could now afford to hire a quality moving company. Reputation and quality of service became paramount for the good moving companies.

As with any industry that provides services to people, there are those that are in it to cheat and swindle. Always do your research. Some feel that the government should regulate the moving industry more like "in the good old days". Big companies can make more money if there is no competition from the little guy.

Moving companies must be licensed with the state, and if they move across the state line, with the federal government as well. There are insurance requirements, and a strict set of rules governing the moving industry. Often the "scams" that make folks cry for more regulation are perpetrated by companies that are already illegal. Existing laws are on the books to deal with criminals.

THE MODERN MOVING INDUSTRY

The moving and storage industry is a fifteen billion dollar per year industry in the united states. Each year about forty million Americans move: eighty-five percent move in state; twelve and a half percent move out of state. Some move themselves while others select a moving company.

According to the BBB, "moving companies" is the fourth most searched category. Everybody wants a good deal and not to be taken advantage of, but a lot of times folks do not take the time to check with the BBB or check the company's credentials. There is no substitute for doing your due diligence.

There are lots of companies to choose from. There are quality movers with fleets of late model moving trucks in every major city in the county. Experienced movers that know how to move all your belongings without damages at a reasonable price.

The moving industry has matured into a capable and effective force in this country. Every day, movers deliver exactly what they have promised: trucks on time, clean cut crews, accurate moving quotes, furniture that is transported and packed with care, and happy customers.

It is worth considering that people (and the nightly news) only want to talk about the few bad apples, ignoring the millions of satisfied customers. The "bad apples" get their business from people that all too often fail to do their due diligence.

Make your move be the best it can be. Hire a quality mover to take the stress out of moving. I hope that you have found this information useful and helpful. Questions and comments are welcomed and appreciated.

Moving is hard enough, make the actual move day easy with the help of a professional crew.

Moving quotes are a call, click, or in-home estimate away.

ABOUT US

MoveCo.net was founded in January 2001 on the simple idea of transparent pricing. The concept of an instant online quoting system gave power to the consumer. Anyone can go online, enter what furniture they want moved, type in the miles from point A to point B, and they have an exact binding move quote. Even today, very few companies place their prices online. As a matter of fact, most moving companies have an online form you can fill out, but then you have to wait for the company to have a sales representative review the itemized list to come up with your moving quote, not MoveCo.net. You get the price for your move as soon as you click "submit". To create a relevant, start up in the highly competitive moving industry, it's important to have a streamlined quoting system.

MoveCo.net has made it our mission to create referrals and repeat business. This has been a long-term goal for our company, and so far, we have achieved this goal. Most people do not move that often, but they do know at least three friends, family members, or coworkers that are planning to move within the next year. These are some of the best customers, because they already know what to expect from MoveCo.net. Standardized pricing via our online quoting system, along with excellent service, is what MoveCo.net's reputation is built on.

MoveCo.net, in addition to pioneering the online quote, also set up a customer feedback board. Our customers can post their experience directly to our website. No other moving company had this feature back in 2001. Now in the year 2017, we are proud to present our Online Video Success Stories to our customers.

Our mission is still the same, to make sure you are not just satisfied with your move, but happy enough to use us again and refer MoveCo.net to your family and friends.

APPENDIX ONE

Your Rights & Responsibilities When You Move in Texas Texas Department of Motor Vehicles Enforcement Division 1(888)368-4689 www.TxDMV.gov

CHOOSING A LICENSED MOVER All household goods motor carriers (movers) operating within Texas are required to have an active certificate of motor carrier registration and abide by the motor carrier rules and regulations under Chapter 218 of title 43, Texas Administrative Code. This includes major van lines, as well as local movers with trucks and trailers. If you are planning to hire a moving company in Texas, we want you to be aware of your rights and responsibilities when choosing a mover. Find more information at www.TxDMV.gov. Choosing Your Mover There are many moving companies out there, so choose your mover carefully. Shop around to find the best prices and services. TxDMV does not regulate fees charged by movers and as a state agency, we will not recommend specific moving companies. However, we do provide a searchable database on our website (www.TxDMV.gov) that you can access to verify whether your mover is properly registered. By contacting the department's Enforcement Division at 1(888) 368-4689, you can obtain information regarding your mover's complaint history. You can also contact the Better Business Bureau (www.bbb.org) for additional information regarding your mover. Proposal for Moving Services Once you've selected your mover, make sure you get everything in writing. Movers are required to provide you with a written proposal prior to loading your items. The proposal may be either a binding proposal (states the exact price of the move) or a not-to-exceed proposal (states the maximum price of the move), and must be signed by both you and the mover. For movers to give you an accurate estimate, you must be clear about the items you want moved and advise them of any special conditions, such as stairs, long carries or elevators that are involved in the move. The proposal should also indicate when payment is due, and what forms of payment are accepted, such as personal checks or credit cards.

Moving Services Contract Your mover is also required to provide you with a moving services contract prior to loading your items. The agreements on the written proposal provided by your mover also become a part of your contract and can actually be one combined document. The contract should contain all the information about your move including your name, the mover's name, the origin and destination points and the amount of the mover's limitation of liability for loss or damage of your property. Be sure all agreements between you and your mover are written into the moving services contract. Do not rely on any verbal agreements. READ ALL DOCUMENTS CAREFULLY BEFORE SIGNING YOUR NAME. DURING YOUR MOVE Mover's Liability All licensed movers have a standard liability of 60 cents per pound article. For example, if a 50–pound television is damaged as a result of a move, the mover is only required to reimburse you $30 (50 lbs. X 0.60 = $30). Some movers will assume a higher level of liability, however, it must be agreed upon by both parties and additional fees may be assessed by the mover. Keep in mind that the mover's limits are not the same as insurance. You, as the shipper, can obtain additional insurance to protect your items. Insurance Some movers may offer to sell you transit insurance, which helps cover loss or damage to your goods, or you can purchase this type of policy from a separate insurance company. Your mover is required to provide you with a copy of the policy and any other appropriate evidence of insurance purchased. Transit insurance is not regulated by TxDMV or the Texas Department of Insurance (TDI), so be sure to carefully read the policy to fully understand your coverage and any deductibles. Inventory of Goods Being Moved Some movers may offer to prepare a descriptive inventory of your items for an additional cost. If an inventory is prepared, it should list all items to be moved and their condition. It should also be signed by both you and the mover prior to and after the move. As with any shipping document, you should review it for accuracy before signing. Important: Inventories are often used during the claims process; inspect your shipment carefully. Make sure all items are accounted for. If there is obvious loss or damage, note this on the inventory at the time of delivery. Pickup and Delivery Dates Advise your mover of any deadlines that you might have with regards to pickup and delivery times. Note these deadlines either on your written proposal or moving services contract. If you are not available at the agreed upon times, contact your mover immediately. If you alter the pickup and/or delivery dates or times you may be charged additional fees. Delivery Your mover must provide you with a completed copy of the moving services contract signed by both you and the mover upon delivery of the shipment. Check the condition of your property and make any notations on the contract document before signing. Paying the Moving Company Remember that the last amended contract or written proposal lists the total price that you will be required to pay at the time of delivery. You should be prepared to pay the maximum amount shown on the written proposal provided by the mover. IN CASE OF A PROBLEM Claims If you have any disputes about charges, or loss or damage to your goods, you need to file a written claim with the mover within 90 days of the delivery date and must include enough information for the mover to investigate your claim along with any specific monetary amounts requested or other solutions you are seeking. Your mover has 20 days to respond acknowledging your claim and has 90 days to pay, deny or make a settlement offer. If your claim involves damaged goods, you should preserve the containers and the damaged goods. The mover has the right to inspect any containers or damaged goods within 30 days of receiving your claim. Important: If your mover does not receive the claim within 90 days of delivery, your claim can be denied.

TxDMV's Role Mediation If you are not satisfied with your settlement offer or your claim is denied, you can contact TxDMV for mediation. A mediation request must be received at TxDMV within 30 days after the mover has responded to your claim with an unsatisfactory offer or denial of your claim, or if you do not receive a response from the mover after 90 days from the original claim. Mediation is conducted by a neutral third party and coordinated by TxDMV at no cost to the shipper. Ideally, mediation will be held by telephone, by written submissions or in person at TxDMV facilities in Austin, Texas. If mediation is unsuccessful, you may pursue the claim in a court of law at your expense. Complaints If you have a complaint against a moving company in Texas, you can file a complaint with TxDMV by: • Going online at: www.TxDMV.gov • Calling us at: 1(888) 368-4689 • Emailing us at: TruckStop@TxDMV.gov Interstate Moves Movers who transport shipments across state lines are regulated by the Federal Motor Carrier Safety Administration (FMCSA). For more information on interstate moving companies or to file a complaint regarding an interstate move, visit: www.protectyourmove.gov or contact: Federal Motor Carrier Safety Administration, www.fmcsa.dot.gov; 1(800) 832-5660. Need more help? Go to www.TxDMV.gov.

APPENDIX TWO

Government and Oversight Organization Contact Information.

IF YOU WANT TO VERIFY A MOVING COMPANY is licensed, or if you have a complaint against a moving company in Texas, contact Tx DMV by going online at: www.TxDMV.gov • Calling at: 1(888) 368-4689 • Emailing at: **TruckStop@TxDMV.gov**

Interstate Movers who transport shipments across state lines are regulated by the Federal Motor Carrier Safety Administration (FMCSA). For more information on interstate moving companies or to file a complaint regarding an interstate move, visit: www.protectyourmove.gov or contact: Federal Motor Carrier Safety Administration, www.fmcsa.dot.gov; 1(800) 832-5660.

American Moving & Storage Association
WWW.PROMOVER.ORG
1611 Duke Street Alexandria, VA 22314
(888) 849-AMSA [2672]

SOUTHWEST MOVERS ASSOCIATION
WWW.MYTEXASMOVER.COM
700 E 11th St Austin, TX 78701
512.476.0107

Better Business Bureau

www.bbb.org/bbb-locator/

APPENDIX THREE
Rental Truck and Moving Supply Contact Info

U-HAUL
www.uhaul.com
To reserve by phone, call
1-800-GO-UHAUL® (1-800-468-4285)

Reservation Date   _____
Truck Rental Cost   _____
Pads/Dollies Rental Cost_____
Quote/Confirmation #_____

Penske Truck Rental
www.pensketruckrental.com
1.844.210.6887

Reservation Date   _____
Truck Rental Cost   _____
Pads/Dollies Rental Cost_____
Quote/Confirmation #_____

Budget Truck
www.budgettruck.com

Reservation Date   _____
Truck Rental Cost   _____
Pads/Dollies Rental Cost_____
Quote/Confirmation #_____

APPENDIX FOUR
HELPFUL PHONE NUMBERS

Old House

My Electric Company_____

My Water Company_____

My Gas Company_____

My Cable Company_____

My Satellite Company_____

My Phone Company_____

My Trash Company_____

New House

My Electric Company_____

My Water Company_____

My Gas Company_____

My Cable Company_____

My Satellite Company_____

My Phone Company_____

My Trash Company_____

My Real Estate Broker_____

My Mortgage Company_____

My Title Company_____

My Home Owner's Association_____

My Handyman_____

My Landscaper_____

My Maid Service_____

My Plumber_____

My AC Repairman_____

My Electrician_____

My Moving Company www.MoveCo.net (972)-250-1100

My Miscellaneous Numbers

_____
_____
_____
_____
_____
_____
_____
_____
_____
_____
_____
_____
_____
_____

APPENDIX FIVE

Change Your Address with the Postal Service.

Go to USPS.com/move to change your address online. This is the preferred method for speed and convenience and you immediately get an email confirmation of the change.

OR

Go to your local post office and request a Movers Guide.

Driver License Renewal and Change of Address.

https://txapps.texas.gov/tolapp/txdl/

1.866.DL-renew (1.866.357.3639)

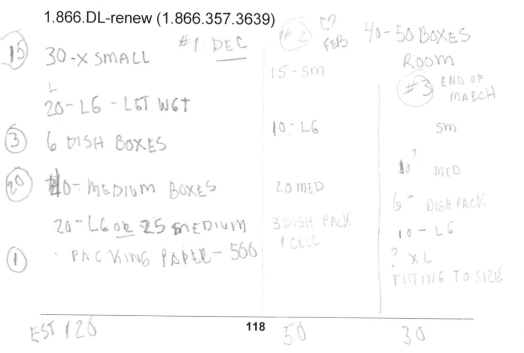

(15) 30-X SMALL   #1 DEC   #2 FEB   40-50 BOXES
                                                          ROOM
   L   15-SM
   20-LG - LST WGT   #3 END OF MARCH

(3) 6 DISH BOXES   10-LG   SM

(20) 40- MEDIUM BOXES   20 MED   10? MED
                          3 DISH PACK   6 - DISH PACK
   20-LG or 25 MEDIUM   1 CELL   10 - LG
(1) · PACKING PAPER - 500   ? XL
                                          FITTING TO SIZE

EST 120   **118**   50   30

APPENDIX SIX

Self-inventory sheet

Note: Put marks next to inventory items, example: (/////) for number of items or a 0 if not applicable. This list can be called, faxed, or e-mailed to the moving company. This list can be used to keep a permanent record and list of all your furniture and boxes.

Appliances

Quantity Description

    AC, Window

    Cooler

    — Ironing Board

    Microwave

    Mop/Broom

    Refrigerator Stainless Steel

    Refrigerator/Freezer Reg.

    Refrigerator/Freezer Sm.

    Stove/Range

    — Vacuum

    Washer/Dryer (if set, list 2)

    Washer/Dryer Front Load (if set, list 2)

Handwritten annotations:
LG MIRRORS – 2
52X 30"
ART – 3
40 X 40
CURTAIN RODS.
— SHOP VAC

Baby Nursery

Quantity Description

    Bassinette

    Bed, Youth

    Changing Table

    Child Chair

    Child Table

    Child Toy, Under 25 Lbs

    Crib

    — Stroller/Car Seat

Bedrooms
Quantity Description

Armoire Oversize   MIRROR

— Armoire Reg.   4 PIECE   + 30 X 72 V

Armoire Sm.

— Bed, Full — (METAL FRAME) ?

Bed, King

Bed, Queen

Bed, Twin

Bridge Bed

Bunk Bed

2 — Cedar Chest/Trunk

3 — Chest of Drawers   40 X 42 / 32 X 29 / 47 X 3

Daybed

Dresser   36 X 30 BOOK SHELVES

Dresser Oversize

Footboard Reg.

Footboard Oversize

Headboard Oversize

Headboard Reg.

3 — Mirror Oversize

— Mirror Reg.

Mirror Sm.

Nightstand

Waterbed (must be drained)

Boxes
Quantity Description

18 X 18 X 28 Dish Pack, Less Than 5.2 Cubic FT and Under 60 LBS

18 X 18 X 24 Large Box, Less Than 4.2 Cubic FT and Under 40 LBS

18 X 18 X 16 Medium Box, Less Than 3.1 Cubic FT and Under 40 LBS

16 1/2 X 12 1/2 Small Box, Less Than 1.5 Cubic FT   35 LB

12 1/2 Wardrobe Box, Less Than 10 Cubic FT and Under 50 LBS
24 X 24 X 34

AMAZON- MATT SOFT MATTRESS BAGS - 32 ^{79} EACH

Garage and Outdoor

Quantity Description

- BBQ/Grill
- Bench
- Bicycle
- Garage Shelves/Cab, Under 60 LBS
- Golf Clubs
- Ladder, Step
- Ladder, Under 10 FT (when closed)
- Mower, Push
- Mower, Ride-On
- Patio Chairs
- Patio End Tables
- Patio Table
- Patio Table Glass
- Patio Umbrella
- Toolbox Lg., Under 120LBS
- Toolbox Sm.
- Tools Lg. (e.g. saw table)
- Tools Sm.
- Weed Eater, Trimmer, Edger, Spreader, Ect.
- Work Bench, Under 6FT

Kitchen and Dining

Quantity Description

- Baker's Rack
- Bar Stool
- Bar, Portable
- Buffet
- China Cabinet
- China Cabinet, 2 Pc.
- Curio Cabinet
- Dining Chairs
- Dining Table
- Dining Table Glass, Less Than 4FT

Handwritten annotations:

ELECTRIC POWER WASH

GARDEN TOOLS

2 LEAF RAKES   SHOVELS - 3
HAND TOOLS
ROOF RAKE

PIPE CLAMPS
60"

2GAL-35LB   2-GRANITE 108EA
AIR COMPRESOR
WOOD CRATE   VISE - 30LB
+20LB
SHOP VAC

TOOL CHEST WHEELS
36 H 30 W
TABLE TOP GRINDER

PORTABLE SEWING
MACHINE

CAST IRON PIPE - 58LB

30 SMALL BOXES
HAND TOOLS

— TODDLER CARSEAT- 2   121   DROPLEAF TABLE   REVISED

Dining Table Glass, Less Than 6FT

Dining Table Lg.

Glass Shelves

Kitchen Table

Tea Cart

Wine Rack

Living Room

Quantity Description

Area Rug

Area Rug, Over 8 FT

2 — Bookcase – SM + 3 LEVEL LAWYER

— Bookcase Oversize

Chair Occasional/Straight

Chair Overstuffed/Recliner

Chair Wingback/Rocker

Chaise Lounge

Coffee/Sofa Table

Coffee/Sofa Table, Glass Top

DVD/CD Rack

End/ Occasional Table

End/Occasional Table, Glass Top

Entertainment Center 1 Pc. Lg.

Entertainment Center 1 Pc. Sm.

Entertainment Center 3 Pc.

Fan/Lamps, (shade must be boxed)

Hall Tree

Ottoman/Footstool

Pictures Under 2 FT

— Pictures Under 4FT

Sofa Loveseat

Sofa Recliner

Sofa Reg.

Sofa Sleeper/Hide-a-bed

Stereo Components/Speakers Reg.

TV 13"-19"

TV 20"-29"

TV 30"-36" — 34" IN BOX

TV 41"-59"

TV 60" -70"

TV Stand

Miscellaneous Other Items

Quantity Description

Exercise Bench, No LBS

Exercise Equipment Standard, Elliptical

Exercise Equipment Standard, Bike

Exercise Equipment Standard, Bow flex

Exercise Equipment Standard, Treadmill

Exercise Equipment Standard, Weight Bench W/ LBS

Exercise Weights/Dumbbells (enter number of LBS)

— Folding Chairs   — 2

Folding Table

Glass Shelves

Glass Top Less Than 2 FT

Glass Top Less Than 4 FT

Glass Top Less Than 6 FT

Glass Top Less Than 8 Ft

Glass Top Less Than 10 FT

Grandfather Clock

Marble Top Less Than 2 FT

Marble Top Less Than 4FT — 33"

Marble Top Less Than 6 FT

Marble Top Less Than 8 FT

Piano Bench

Piano Upright (downstairs)

Piano, Baby Grand (downstairs)

Plants Fake Less Than 6 FT

Plants Less Than 60 LBS

Plants Small

Statue, Less Than 40LBS

Vase

Office

Quantity Description

Computer Components

Conference Table Reg.

Copier/Printer Sm.

Credenza

Desk Chair

Desk Computer

Desk Extension

 Desk Hutch

Desk Mat

Desk Reg.

Desk Roll Top

Desk Secretary

Desk Sm.

Desk Office

Drafting Table

File Cab. 2 Drawer

File Cab. 2 Drawer Lateral

File Cab. 4 Drawer

File Cab. 4 Drawer Lateral

Printer/Fax Stand

1 - BENCH

APPENDIX SEVEN

(reprinted with permission from the MoveCo.net website)

"Tips and Tricks Before Move Day"

We appreciate each and every one of our customers who choose us for their moving needs. Below is a list of Tips and Tricks that will help you with your upcoming move. Please go through them and see how prepared you are for your move.

For your information, here are some things we cannot move: cleaning supplies, gas or propane containers, fertilizer or potting soil in bags; anything else that could explode, leak or spill inside the truck.

1. Have all personal items cleared off the top and out of furniture before move day; have walkways clear of furniture and boxes.

2. If dusting furniture, do not use "Pledge" or any sort of polish- DRY DUST.

3. File change of address forms with the Post Office

4. Arrange for transfers of school records, if needed.

5. Make arrangements for storage (either with MoveCo.net's Climate Controlled Storage or private storage), if necessary. Place Baking Soda inside refrigerators and freezers to reduce odors.

6. Check to see if you need any moving permits where you are moving. (Examples:
Certificates of Insurance, floor protection, etc.)

7. If you are moving to an apartment, reserve the elevator preferably with a 'Hold Door Key' if available.

8. Make child/pet care arrangements for moving day.

9. Drain power equipment of oil and gas. Drain water hoses. Drain your waterbed. Clean inside of and unhook propane connections from BBQ grills and smokers.

10. Have outdoor recreational items disassembled and clean. (B-ball goals drained and disassembled; play sets, etc. disassembled and clean from dirt, mud, or insects.)

11. Have items that require disassembly already disassembled prior to move day. Movers will disassemble and reassemble standard beds, mirrors on dressers and appliances.

12. Do not water plants 2 days prior to moving.

13. Defrost your refrigerator and freezer if moving more than 50 miles, or if storing.

14. If you have not hired MoveCo.net to pack your belongings, and are packing yourself, please have all boxes SEALED, properly labeled, and ready to move.

15. If moving to two locations ie apt/storage color code your items. Use Neon Masking Tape.

16. Set aside or label items that will be moved by you so they will not be loaded in the truck. Pack a box of items that will be needed first at the new house, if any. Label the box "Load Last, Open First".

17. Be sure someone is at both locations to answer any questions the movers may have. Note utility readings.

18. Bring all items being moved down from the attic prior to move day. (Movers cannot go up into attics for MoveCo.net Insurance purposes.)

19. Empty all large furniture (armoires, desks, file cabinet, china cabinets, buffets, etc.) prior to moving. You can leave only have light clothes in dressers and chest of drawers for move day.

20. Supervise loading and unloading, note any possible damages on the final paperwork.

21. Have payment ready before the crew unloads the truck at your new home.

22. Payment accepted in forms of: check (upon approval), Cashier's Check, Cash or Credit Card only.

23. Sleep Number Bed Prep for Moving: Air up your mattress then, unplug the hoses and cap the both inner tubes. Caps can be found inside of the mattress. Sleep number mattress have a zipper on the top left side.

24. Shipping bolts are used to secure the front load Washer Machines, so that the drum doesn't move. Please make sure your Shipping bolts are installed on your washer on move day, or inside your washer for the movers to install.

25. Make sure all Jewelry, Guns, and Ammo is put up before the packers/movers arrive on pack/move day. (Moving companies are not allowed to touch or move these items)

Thank you for taking the time to review our Tips and Tricks for a successful move.

APPENDIX EIGHT
CONTACT INFORMATION

www.MoveCo.net
800-590-0928
1596 North Mill Street
Lewisville, Texas 75057

TXDOT #006044279C   MC #541225   USDOT #1432374

MoveCo.net You Tube Channel
https://www.youtube.com/channel/UCPmxNlaBQlo0DqR49gB
PGXw

MoveCo.net BBB Page
https://www.bbb.org/dallas/business-
reviews/movers/moveconet-in-lewisville-tx-43001520

MoveCo.net Facebook Page
https://www.facebook.com/MoveCo.Net/

MoveCo.net YouTube: Tips and Tricks Playlist:
https://www.youtube.com/watch?v=8deNqnjhHqs&list=PLYzqz
3taplZUxo29XWgfgmRQFz-5UZp5v

"We are a full service moving company.
To what level do you want us to serve
you?"

www.MoveCo.net

Office: 972 250-1100
Toll Free: 800 590-0928

APPENDIX NINE
(Reprinted with permission from the MoveCo.net website)

Our Standards

When you are looking for a moving company, here are some helpful things to consider. This is MoveCo.net's standard. This is what sets MoveCo.net apart from the competition.

- Over 200 Customer Video Reviews from 2014-2016 on our official MoveCo.net YOU TUBE channel.
- We maintain an online feedback board for our customers to post their comments.
- We have guaranteed move prices.
- We have guaranteed pickup and delivery dates.
- Our customers have exclusive use of our trucks, we do one move at a time.
- Our fleet of trucks is tracked by GPS. We know where our trucks are at all times.
- We maintain a Texas Department of Motor Vehicle (TX DMV) registration number.
- We maintain a US Department of Transportation (US DOT) registration number.
- We maintain membership in good standing with the Southwest Movers Association.
- We maintain membership in good standing with the Better Business Bureau.
- We maintain membership in good standing with the Chamber of Commerce.
- We have well over 100 years in combined experience.
- All of our drivers have at least 2 years' experience (and many with much more).
- We maintain $300,000 worth of commercial auto liability insurance.
- We maintain $100,000 worth of Cargo Insurance.

- We have an in-house policy to Repair/Replace anything we damage within reason.
- We maintain a $25,000 Bond.
- We comply with all state advertising rules and regulations.
- We maintain and enforce an associate dress code.
- We maintain and enforce a formal alcohol/drug testing program for all associates.
- We maintain and enforce a formal associate conduct policy.
- We have conducted background searches on all our movers.
- We comply with all other state and federal regulatory requirements.
- We maintain late model trucks and moving equipment.
- We have itemized prices -no hourly moves, you pay for what is done not "clock watchers".
- Upfront pricing, you can go to our website and get an online itemized quote.

Notes

Notes

Notes

Notes

Notes

Notes